La Cucina della mia Bisnonna

— *The Kitchen of My Great Grandmother* —

Lynn Tiramani

Copyright © 2019 by Lynn Tiramani.

All rights reserved. No part of this publication may be reproduced, distributed, or transmitted in any form or by any means, including photocopying, recording, or other electronic or mechanical methods, without the prior written permission of the author, except in the case of brief quotations embodied in critical reviews and certain other noncommercial uses permitted by copyright law.

Printed in the United States of America.

Library of Congress Control Number: 2018904036

ISBN		
	Paperback	978-1-64361-782-4
	Hardback	978-1-64361-783-1
	eBook	978-1-64361-784-8

Westwood Books Publishing LLC
10389 Almayo Ave, Suite 103
Los Angeles, CA 90064

www.westwoodbookspublishing.com

Contents

Introduction 1
My Inspiration 5
My Godmother's Famous Chicken Soup 41
The Two Ladies Spinach Soup 43
Minestrone (Italian Vegetable Soup) 45
Burdetto (Soup with Eggs) 47
Pasta with Beans (Fagoli) 49
Louisa's Marinara Sauce 51
Homemade Tomato Sauce for Sauce 55
Nonna's Sweet and Sour Sauce 57
Porcini Mushroom Sauce 61
Garlic and Oil Sauce 64
Tripe 66
Chicken Cacciatori 68
Polenta 71
Ravioli's with Mushroom Filling 74
Ravioli with Butternut Squash Filling .77
Ravioli's with Spinach and Ricotta 80
Tortolini in Brodo (Soup) 83
Risotto 86
Pasta 90
Torta 93
Fritatta 95
Grandfather Giovanni's Lamb Recipe .98
Great Grandmother Maria's Veal 101

Louisa's Rainy Day Chicken Recipe........................105
Nonna's Cod Fish Recipe................................107
Mom's Fish Filet Recipe................................109
Broccoli with an Italian Twist 111
Carrots 112
Peppers Alla Dina 113
Ossobuco 114
Simple Roast Beef 116
Asparagus Italian Style 117
Sweet Potatoes with a Nutmeg Twist 118
Mushrooms Alla Dina 119
Tony's Peasant Potatoes 120
Nonna Louisa's Cutlets 121
Nonna Linda's Eggplant 123
Louisa's Spare Rib 124
Nonna's Lentil Soup 126
Fried Potatoes with Rosemary 127
Fried Potatoes with Bay Leaves 128
Stuffed Mushrooms......................................129
Shrimp Alla San Micheal 130
Gnocchi 131
Sauce for Gnocchi......................................132
Bow Tie Cookies..133
Crostata...134
Sabgione 135

Introduction

Being of Italian descent, the definition of my original sin was being born with a decadent desire for food. No form of baptismal water could wash away my original sin. I was brought into the world by a mother, Louisa whose canvas was her kitchen. Like an artist, her mastery of marrying different foods with various flavors made her equivalent to Picasso in my eyes. It's a compliment that is often afforded my mother, Louisa but that she quickly dismisses as a mere passion that bears little importance.

As a child, I was introduced quite early to the culinary delights that called Northern Italy their home. A cuisine which had been foreshadowed until recently by its comparable Southern counterpart. As its existence came out from behind the darkness, many of the partakers, composed primarily of family and friends, had their plates pleasantly introduced to both the savory and intellectual brilliance of how all these ingredients were combined. Even the most skeptical critics were pleasantly surprised and, upon taste and review, gave it four stars. Their amazement of how my mother orchestrated the marriage of the many different flavors warranted them making a return engagement to the confines of my mother's dining room.

Especially during the holidays, the majority of my formidable years were spent filled with exasperated anticipation and whining impatience for the impending performance my mother would give in the kitchen, especially during the holiday season. At Christmas, most normal children would often do chores for a week to obtain the opportunity to have front row seats in around the tree. They were willing to pay top allowance money to have the feel of the red seats, similar to the ones at Madison Square Garden. Not me, I wanted to be in the orchestra pit of my mother's kitchen. I often felt as if I was sitting right near Jeffrey Lyons and we were both commissioned to write a review regarding my mother's cooking for the prestigious *"New York Times."* In the eyes of an unseasoned and unblemished critic, such as myself, I often wrote that this feast would garner raves worthy of Academy Award consideration.

My mother, Louisa, bearing the discipline of Bob Fosse and the perfectionism of Andrew Lloyd Weber, was certain to make sure that the understudies, such as leeks, celery, oil, and butter, were limber and perfectly entwined so they would marinate with the other performers. The other performers for most of her recipes were the main staples of onions, rosemary or porcini mushrooms. She always made sure these ingredients lived up to her expectations so they would sustain themselves through the four acts of all her various culinary operas. These four acts included the antipasto, pasta, main course, and dessert. It was vital that these ingredients were void of all nerves and blemishes. As always, her critics consisted of various members of my family, who needed to have their dull palates stimulated until the curtain came down. When the curtain came down, my mother received what was comparable to a five curtain call.

I traveled this culinary adventure quite frequently during the crossroads of my life. Now, as I fear my chronological presence on this earth begins to lessen, it is at this time, I am compelled to take various companions to bear witness to the sights, sounds and smells that comprise this wonderful gastronomical flight. I extend my invitation to you, the reader, to bear witness so that you may assist me in proclaiming the gospel of this secular cuisine primarily practiced in the Northern section of Italy. Let us begin the conversion.

The conversion begins with a warning. This cookbook is not designed for the preparation in minutes chef, but for the chef whose life would mimic those of a priest. Cooking alert, this is not a thirty-minute meal cookbook. It is for people whose view of cooking mimics a priest's view of religion. As opposed to a dedication to a religion and a people, your spiritual allegiance from this day on would be to the mechanisms that create all these mouth-watering wonders. As opposed to a dedication to a religion and a people, your spiritual allegiance from this day on will be to the mechanisms that create all these mouth-watering wonders.

In the next few pages, you will journey with me to the birthplace of where these gastronomic masterpieces were developed into their mouthwatering canvases. Like many of the canvases created by many of the great painters. Though extremely difficult to duplicate, one taste or one look will propel you to run, not walk, to your kitchen. Like Michelangelo with the Sistine Chapel, any doubts of incompletion will be dispelled.

My Inspiration

Great-Grandmother, Maria: The Main Architect of the Cuisine

My great grandmother, Maria Pinazzi, was the primary architect of the recipes which are the foundation for this wonderful cuisine. Maria made her grand entrance into the world in 1870. She was born in the little town of Gropparello in the Province of Piacenza. Piacenza is located in the Emilia-Romagna Region. Emilia-Romagna is located wide plain south of the Po River. It is to the west and includes the provinces of Piacenza, Parma, Reggio, Emilia, Modena, Ferrara and the western part of the province of Bologna. Emilia-Romagna region is also the home to one of the first universities in the world, the University of Bologna. The automobile companies of Ferrari, Lamborghini, Maserati, De Tomaso, and Ducati call this region their home. Piacenza's claim to fame is that it has the great distinction of being the foremost cultural center in times of peace and the primary place of focus in times of conflict. It is also known throughout the rest of the world for its production of seasoned and salted pork products. The most prominent specialties are pancetta (rolled seasoned pork belly, salted and spiced), coppa (seasoned pork neck, containing less fat than pancetta, matured at least for six months) and salami (chopped pork meat flavored with spices and wine, and made in sausages). The main dialect spoken in Piacenza is Piacentine. Although with the advent of the 20th century, the Piacentine dialect has experienced a steady decline and is presently a nonexistent form of communication among the locals.

During Maria's childhood, about 1,000 people called Gropparello their home. Most of Italy, at this time in history, was extremely poor and viewed the government as an absent parent. The economic situation which gripped the country forced about 26 million Italians to migrate to the United States between the years of 1880 to 1920. The main occupation of those who chose to remain was farming. The fruits of the land gave the people an income as well as nourishment. They grew everything from corn to wheat. Many of the residents also had wineries as another form of revenue. However, Maria realized at a young age that she was not exceedingly fond of the concept of dancing on grapes, and, therefore, did not pursue this additional business later in life. Instead, she would ultimately develop a passion for creating masterpieces through the magic of her wooden stove. Among the instruments she used to create them, were heavy cast iron pots, long-handled spatulas, and spoons. Through much practice, she was able to merger meager ingredients into mouthwatering pleasures which would become the chisel that enabled her to destroy the poverty which she was born into. This cooking aptitude allowed her to open a successful restaurant that still continues today.

From the very beginning, Maria's life would be marred with tremendous sadness. Maria would never know her mother. Her mother, Philomena, passed away a month after she was born. Her father Giovanni, later remarried. This union not only produced eight step-siblings but a step-mother who suffered from the wicked step mother syndrome. Maria would be forced into a Cinderella-like existence. Like her storybook counterpart, she assumed all the household duties and was only afforded her own little corner. Her parents, Giovanni and his Angela, amassed a great deal of land through the course of their lives. Upon her parents' demise, the land was equally left to her eight step-siblings and nothing was left to Maria. This would prove to be the final and most lasting, heart-wrenching indignity in a line of many. Ultimately, this indignity was the propelling fuel that ignited the desire in her to achieve and prove her worth. Maria proved her strength and determination by successfully running her restaurant and at the same time raising her own eight children through the most economically trying times brought on primarily by Italy's participation in World War I. World War I, was a war which was primarily centered in Europe. It began on July 28, 1914 and would end on November 11, 1918. It is often referred to and remembered as "The Great War to end all wars." Italy's allies in this war were the United Kingdom, France, and the Russian Empire. Not only did the war cause the economy to falter, but 650,000 soldiers would be led to an untimely death to their maker. Of those who were spared this fate, 950,000 were wounded and 250,000 were crippled for life. Even in the wake of all this mayhem and horror, Maria never gave up and always strived to make life better for herself and others no matter how difficult the circumstances. Maria would prove her strength and determination by successfully running her restaurant and, at the same time, raising eight children through the most economically trying times. Maria was the blueprint of what we consider today a working woman. You could say she was a woman before her time. Quite simply, Maria was a renaissance woman.

My great grandmother, Maria married my great grandfather, Giovanni Gugliemetti at the age of twenty. This union, like her father's second marriage, produced eight children. She had five boys and three girls. They settled in a humble abode in Piacenza which would ultimately house the dining room which would be converted into a restaurant. Despite the tepid relationship with her stepmother, my great grandmother, Maria made sure her children were aware of her existence and often took them to see her. My great grandmother, Maria was not only proficient in cooking but was also gifted in the workings of the farm and the financial running of the household. It was through her intimate relationship with currency and the lack of it, that she realized that another form of raising it was vital. This reality turned her dining room into an eating establishment. As soon as my grandmother, Linda and her siblings came of age, they too would assist in the running of the restaurant. My great grandmother, Maria died when my mother, Luisa was six months old. My mother, Louisa would often lament to me that it was one of the biggest short changes of her life that she never had the opportunity to establish a relationship with her. She believes that Maria's great passion for food was spiritually transferred into her being. Therefore, her grandmother, Maria's legacy of cooking continues to live on through the generations and will continue for many generations to come.

In the early days, my great grandmother, Maria's rustic establishment looked like a medieval castle gone awry. It housed ten tables accompanied by five sets of chairs. The tables resembled something that was purchased from the now-defunct five and dime stores which flooded 1960's America. Despite its various cosmetic shortcomings, her establishment succeeded due to the magic that was created in her sparse kitchen. It was a kitchen which produced such treasures as soup, risotto, lamb, ravioli and vegetables. Each meal would be finished with a plain pound cake called, "PANNE DOLCE" (Sweet cake). Word of her restaurant traveled quickly, because of the town's small population. The restaurant was open every day. Sunday's was her busiest day. The faithful would hurriedly scramble to her restaurant after mass. After listening to the priest's preaching about the need to seek forgiveness, the parishioners were in dire need of a calming and delectable meal to assist them in completing their penance with even more sincerity. The rest of the week, her many patrons were primarily peasants, hunters and her export neighbors from England and France. Her husband, Giovanni often played the part of her sue chef in the kitchen and at times, would even assist her with the cooking. My great grandfather, Giovanni would often give her pointers on various ingredients for certain recipes. My great grandfather, Giovanni learned his trade by being his mother's constant shadow in the kitchen. His other occupations consisted of farmer and butcher. Giovanni was the town butcher. Through the years, Giovanni mastered the art of making homemade salami. Giovanni's proficiency in making various salami enabled him to compete in various competitions in France later in life. Giovanni would eventually win two gold medals. My great grandfather, Giovanni died in 1944 of cancer.

As each new dawn brought light to another day, the brilliance of the sunlight provided both the physical and mental motors which held residence within Maria to ignite and enable my grandmother to get up each day and help her to commence her adventure in securing the ingredients for the day's feast. Often, due to the economic climate of the times, they would be minimal. On one particular day, a patron requested a bowl of soup. Mind you, he did not request the commonplace chicken soup but something quite different. Luckily, all good cooks are gifted with attributes such as resourcefulness and imagination to please even the most difficult patrons. Trust me, as you will travel with me through this book, you will find that my great grandmother possessed these qualities in spades. Tapping into both these allies, Maria, called upon one of her most reliable culinary friends whose allegiance through the course of her life remained unfailing. This, of course, is tomato sauce.

As my great grandmother, Maria opened the doors of her restaurant, she proceeded to the little patch of land which occupied the space behind her little establishment. This piece of soil grew the nirvana which was the base for her soup and many of her other recipes. As Maria picked the beautiful red tomatoes, she was often propelled to marvel how this round creation turned dull recipes into unforgettable ones. Upon completion of this task, she proceeded into the kitchen to wash them. Maria would cut them into quarters and cook them until they were reduced to liquid form. Maria would then use a primitive strainer and with a spoon mash the tomatoes. Meanwhile, in a separate pot, she combined oil, parsley, and garlic and simmered them together. Maria poured the tomato sauce in the pot with these ingredients. A strand of the basil which would bring life to these simple ingredients. Maria cooked this mixture on medium heat with water for about fifteen minutes. At this point, she added the pasta. The pasta should cook about 10 to 12 minutes or taste. As Maria completed this recipe, Maria wondered if the other patron who had ventured in quite innocently, would upon completion of the meal, loss the directions to her venue or come back for a repeat performance.

At that moment, Maria's thoughts were suddenly disrupted by a loud booming voice. Most of the natives were forced to deal with this unwelcomed, yet charming, characteristic of many older Italian men. My father, Stefano personally forced me to become quite accustomed to. The patron, although a longtime resident of this little corner of the earth, never bothered to partake in a meal served at my great grandmother's establishment before. Known to be, by all his neighbors of a skeptical nature, he finally had to see for himself what all the fuss was about. Eager to reach him, unfortunately, Maria's advancing age often prohibited her from reaching her destination in a timely fashion. Once in his presence, his impatience was quite apparent. My great grandmother, Maria apologized profusely and seated him. Maria immediately presented him with a glass of homemade wine. Maria then marched to her sanctuary and began to cook the pasta which was the final ingredient of her edible potion. While the pasta was cooking, Maria prepared a salad of raw escarole with a little bit of oil and salt. After a final taste, she poured it gingerly into a bowl and placed it on a tray. Maria dressed it with accessories such as a bowl of grated cheese and a few slices of homemade bread and, of course, the salad.

Maria proceeded into the dining area; her heart trembled with an uneven beat. For the first time, Maria felt uncertainty in her culinary capabilities. Maria was serving a recipe which was void of all royalty and unfortunately, Maria was serving an individual who felt he should be treated as such. Maria approached the table and placed it before him. His doubtful laced gaze caused the pit of my great grandmother, Maria's insides to sink. He demanded that Maria stay until his savory glands had completed their first interaction to her peasant fare. As he finished swallowing the food, he looked up at Maria, a brilliant smile, which could brighten the room emanated from his lips. A sigh, which was embedded in her soul, was released by the relief his reaction had brought her. He informed Maria that her genius with minimal ingredients would enable her to hold court with other culinary giants. Characteristically, as with all Italians, there was an automatic movement of his hand as expressed that his admiration of her creation. Maria thanked him but indicated his high praise was unwarranted for a cuisine which would be a minor footnote in a four-star restaurant. Again, as all Italians do, they continued to argue the point until exasperation on my great grandmother Maria's part finally forced her to agree with him.

An hour later, and a bottle of wine consumed, the patron finally dismissed himself. Once again, he thanked Maria and let her know that he would be back. He also stated that he would go out and proclaim to those who were unaware, about the tiny establishment that produced such big flavors. In the weeks ahead, his echoed sentiment spread through Italy and beyond. The great demand brought both expansions to the restaurant and eventually permanent employment for the generations that followed.

It was at this juncture that his little piece of culinary real estate located in Pradovera, Italy matured into an establishment which, to this day, consists of a bar, dining area, an expanded kitchen, and two bedrooms. The two bedrooms were installed to provide a haven for weary travelers, hunters, and nomads who happen to pass through with no place to stay. Or even, if they just wanted a few days, to find solace from the demands that plagued them every day. Often, at the end of their stay, they would request written instructions for the recipes that were presented before them. The request was politely denied and often accompanied with a smile and a bottle of homemade wine. Though initially disappointed, the patron was immediately pacified with just one sip of this nectar. For all these reasons, and many others, this very humble eatery continues to thrive even today.

My great grandmother, Maria continued to be the engine which ran the everyday operation. This would continue until her 50th Birthday. The dawn of her 50th Birthday brought a malfunctioning heart which would plague Maria until her demise at the age of 65. During her last fifteen years, Maria handed down the reigns to the next generation. The next generation, being her son, Casimiro and with it schooled him on the various aspects of how to run the operation properly. At the end of the day, her weak heart forced her to be carried up the stairs to bed each night. A fact which brought a very independent and prideful woman a great deal of dismay until her death in 1935.

It was in 1960 that the embryonic cosmetic state of the restaurant was converted into a small bed and breakfast. Its confines housed a bar, a delicatessen, four bedrooms and a spacious room which often served as a dining room and a dance hall. It has the capacity to hold about two to five hundred people. Future generations continued to be weaned on the culinary treasurers which initially emanated from this small kitchen. Families would often come to celebrate their lives special moments by partaking in the feasts that were created by my great grandmother's wand. Although the restaurant would continue in the hands of future generations, form Casimiro to his son, Luigi. Luigi would own it until 2016. Although the restaurant would continue in the hands of future generations, they would enhance but never stray far from the culinary roots that helped to grow its foundation.

Though, Maria is long gone, not only her culinary lesson but her lessons on how hard work and treating the masses with great respect continue to live on through the generations that were fortunate enough to be born from her family tree. Primarily those family members, that everyday enable her legacy to live on through the continuation of the running of her establishment. Now, you the reader will be afforded a glimpse of the many treasures that were composed many years ago in a nondescript kitchen.

La Cucina della mia Bisnonna

My Grandmother, Linda - The Enhancer

My grandmother, Linda Gugliemetti was born on December 29, 1897. My grandmother, Linda was the oldest among the girls in the family. Linda was born in Farini. Farini is west of Bologna and about 40 Kilometers Southwest of Piacenza. As of December 2004, there were about $1,744.00 who inhabited that piece of land. Linda was about 5'5 and had dirty blonde hair and grey-blue eyes. Linda had four brothers and three sisters. During her childhood, Linda did not attend school after the third grade, because of the terminally hard economic situation, she grew up in. The schoolhouse that Linda ventured to each day, looked like an 1800's backwoods cabin which had taken its toll by nature. When a family had eight mouths to feed, all hands were busy putting food on the table. For many children at that time, education was an inconvenient interruption to helping the family earn a living. Therefore, it was only tolerated and not embraced as a means of bettering yourself. The elders felt that if a child learned to nurture the earth with enough expertise to produce the great treasures that graced the table that was education enough. My grandmother, Linda and her siblings would follow suit and spend the majority of their childhood toiling in the dirt.

When my grandmother Linda was a teenager, she took over some of the cooking duties although she possessed a liking and was very adequate in the various workings of the kitchen, Linda did not have the great desire or passion for concocting culinary magic. These feelings would have to be put aside for as her mother, Maria's chronological age heightened, she needed her daughter, Linda's assistance in the kitchen. Her brother and sisters would join the party later as well. Linda gave up her position in the restaurant kitchen when she married my grandfather Marco Gugliemetti on June 23, 1934.

My grandmother Linda and grandfather Marco were childhood sweethearts. Though their love had fizzled in their teenage years, the spark rekindled later in life. My mother, Louisa was born on April 12, 1935. My mother, Louisa often expressed that she felt like a tolerated, unwelcomed visitor. The presence of love towards my mother, Louise was totally devoid in the space which she occupied with her parents.

In the 1930's the world was marred in an economic depression. Italy was one of the countries that were hit particularly hard. My grandfather, Marco wanting to provide a better life for his family, decided to venture to the shores of America and set his sights on amassing a treasure to support his little family. He planted his first roots in East Harlem, New York. Harlem is an extremely large section in the Northern part of New York City. Ever since the 1920's Harlem has been a major African-American residential, cultural and business center. It was initially a Dutch Village, which was named after the city of Haarlem in the Netherlands. East Harlem, where my grandfather resided, was primarily composed of Italian immigrants. East Harlem's claim to fame was that it was the prime location of the Genovese crime family. It proved to be the perfect location for my grandfather, Marco. The familiarity had made him feel as if the traditions, language and mannerisms of the land of his birth, had accompanied him to his new home. This made the transition easier. My grandfather, Marco would not see his family for another 12 years.

While my grandfather, Marco was away attempting to build his fortune in America, my mother, Louise and grandmother, Linda shared a home with my mother's uncle, and her grandparents, Guiseppi and Louisa Gugliemetti. Twelve other people lived in the same house. During the day, while my mother, Louisa was at school, my grandmother, Linda worked the farm. Eventually, my mother, Linda, like my grandmother, was also forced to leave school early and work on the farm. It was also during this time that my mother, Louisa began building her skills in becoming the proficient cook she is today.

My Mother, Louisa: The Keeper of The Flame

My mother was born in the little town of Farini on April 12, 1935. Farini is located in the Province of Piacenza, Italy. Piacenza is in the Region of Emilia-Romagna. The exact location of Farini is 140 Kilometers west of Bologna and about 40 kilometers southwest of Piacenza. These are the following municipalities which Farini boarders, Bardi, Bettola, Coli, Ferriere and Morfasson. As was the custom and due to the extreme miles, which separated my grandmother, Linda's family and the nearest hospital, my mother was brought into this world through the capable hands of a midwife. The house where my mother, Louisa lived was shared with 14 additional people. My great grandmother**, Maria Grassi** who was my grandfather's mother, would be my mother's main caretaker, while my grandmother, Linda worked the farm. A way in which my grandmother would earn a living was to harvest the rice. Her main job was to pull the herbs which grow with the rice. Rice grows in the same manner in which wheat grows.

Unfortunately, in financially stifled times, education was not the main priority. My mother, Louisa's education would cease at the end of third grade. At the age of eight like many of her friends, my mother, was forced to work the farm, while the rest of the family tried to derive a living from the scarce jobs that afforded them an existence. My mother, Louisa's day would begin at seven in the morning and ended at seven at night. It consisted of feeding the chickens and milking the cows. She then took the cows to the pasture to eat and exercise. It was during these times that my mother, Louisa's thoughts traveled through another meadow. A meadow of despair which was brought on by the inability to further her education. My mother, Louisa knew education would be the only key to unlock the chains of poverty which were so tightly tied around her being.

Also, during this time, like the rest of Europe, Italy was playing host to an unwelcomed guest, World War II. The barrage of bombs that decided to plant themselves in the fields forced the residents to retreat to the basements which lived beneath their humble dwellings. The guests consisted of German soldiers whose many war activities consisted of routinely causing havoc by killing the Partisans. The Partisans were opposed to the Fascist Government which was in place. The German soldiers also welcomed themselves to the meager food supplies that kept the populace alive and took care of their manly desires by raping the young woman. This course of action took place between 1940 to 1945. As you can surmise by these writings, these people were not spared any of the casualties that comprise the ingredients for the recipe of what war is made of.

During the course of my own childhood, war was not a dinner table discussion. In fact, it was often dismissed as a part of the past that just happened long ago. But there was one story, one glimmer of light in a time of darkness, which my mother, Louisa was happy to relay to me and my brother.

It was the middle of the war; my mother recalls the year as 1943. Her and the rest of the people that composed her little town, hid three British soldiers in the woods that surrounded her town. They were kept alive each day by the meager rations of food which were brought to them by this little band of people. Years after the war was over, these soldiers brought their families back to let them meet the people whose generosity and fearlessness gave them the opportunity to survive the perils of war.

Today, the little piece of land in which my mother, Louisa spent her younger years is basically comprised of summer houses. These summer houses are owned by the grandchildren of many of her contemporaries. In the winter, the town resembles a ghost town right out of 1800 America.

The roots of the introduction to this cuisine into my life first began with the arrival of a shy, intrepid filled, though extremely excited, young woman who made her debut appearance on the shores of this land in February 1949. Upon her arrival, my mother, Louisa was relieved to finally have completed a two-week journey which was plagued with nausea filled days primarily prompted by the rough seas which usually accompanied her form of transportation. Those feelings were quickly dispelled and her physical being was better as her feet touched the soil of her new home. It was at that moment; she happily recalled the reasons for leaving the security of her native land to the uncertainly which lay ahead of her. The promise of a new life and the excitement of finally meeting the father she had never known. Her father, Marco left her and my grandmother when my mother was six months old. My grandfather, Marco's main objective for leaving was to venture to a land which would not only enable his immediate family to prosper but also future generations that would continue his family tree. Little did his family know, success in this endeavor had totally eluded my grandfather, Marco during the fourteen years since his arrival in America. He instead befriended the bottle. This companion would stifle any thought or realization of a successful life.

As my mother, Louisa's feet touched the soil of her new home, she was welcomed by her cousin, John and not far behind him was her father, Marco who for the first fourteen years of her life was an enigma. As my grandfather appeared from behind my cousin Paul, both my grandfather and my mother meekly introduced themselves to each other. Due to my grandfather, Marco's absence, my mother was unable to harness or nurture the emotions that usually develop between a father and daughter. My mother, Louisa was immune to all these feelings, and, therefore, the maturation of these emotions was never given the opportunity to grow. Her cousin, John upon the realization of the discomfort between them, immediately motioned them to the car to commence the journey that would lead her to her new life.

John was my mother's first cousin. He was born in 1921. When his mother left, his father became both his mother and father. His education went no further than the Eighth Grade. He would go on to work in construction. He would marry and have a son and a daughter.

My mother, Louisa's very humble abode was located in upper Manhattan on 104th and Third Avenue. Her apartment was on the first floor. It was composed of three rooms, a kitchen, a living room and a bedroom. There was a pull-out couch in the living room. This was the sleeping instrument in which a 14-year-old girl would harness her dreams each night. As they entered the apartment, my mother and grandmother, both having what could be characterized as compulsive obsessive cleanliness, were mortified by what was presented to them. Upon her review of the apartment, my mother was compelled to ask her father if he found a lost pig. My grandmother, Linda proceeded to verbally chastise my grandfather for his negligent attention to the upkeep of his apartment. A wave of sadness engulfed the faces of both my mother and grandmother, as my grandfather, continued to take them on a tour of their new home. Not long afterward, both my mother and grandmother were brought to the realization that my grandfather, Marco failed miserably in the cleanliness department. As the days went on, my mother and grandmother would be confronted with the reality that my grandfather's loneliness and insecurity had propelled him to squander his earnings on his relentless inner addiction, alcohol. An addiction that since his introduction to the new land had had been the crutch that enabled him to endure the loneliness and guilt of leaving his family that resided within him. The local liqueur store appreciated his daily contributions to its upkeep. As my mother and grandmother were confronted with these sad truths, the happiness and anticipation that accompanied them and willed them through their rough two-weeks journey were detonated. Despite these feelings, my grandmother and mother chose to take an optimistic view. Both, quickly dispelled these feelings, instead choosing to possess an optimistic point of view believing that somewhere over their defaulted rainbow would eventually find their blue skies.

The individuals who resided in my mother Louisa's neighborhood was primarily of Italian and Irish descent. My mother also had the great fortune of being surrounded by many cousins. Both the presence of her cousins and those of her countryman brought a comfort level that helped to ease the transition. Their stories of the old country and the family laced her difficult times with laughter and proved to be the perfect sedative to enable her to conquer the obstacles that confronted her daily.

Shortly upon settling in, my mother enrolled in Margaret Knox Junior High School. She was placed in a classroom which was composed of other individuals who shared a common bond with my mother. They too had ventured from other lands seeking a better life. Although the language barrier proved to be a hindrance at times, she refused to let the matter of different languages derail her. My mother, quickly decided that it was through the course of action, as opposed to words, that she would develop friendships with her other classmates. As always, a helping hand, compassion, and caring is a language that is universally understood. My mother's sheer will and determination ultimately enabled her to succeed in both mastering the language and developing friendships that remain even to this day.

Meanwhile, as was the case with many immigrants, her parents were willing to do any form of labor that was available to them. My grandmother, Linda ultimately worked as a seamstress during the day and the night labored as a cleaning lady at a local music school. It was her job to make sure that the dust which accumulated during the day never saw the light of another day. My grandmother, Linda was often commended by her supervisors on how gifted she was in making the school look as if the equipment, upon completion of her cleaning, the next day, looked as if had been newly purchased. My grandfather, Marco tooled as a laborer. The majority of the laborers at the time were comprised of Italian immigrants. This fact proved to be the biggest initiative in my grandfather, Marco becoming a laborer. For two years, my mother, Louisa's little family continued this manner of living until an unwelcomed and destructive visitor, decided to befriend my grandmother. The visitor, she would find, would be cancer. This news, unfortunately, would prove to dictate the direction in which my mother's life would travel during her teenage years. A journey in which for the rest of her formidable years, would soon force her life to be devoid of any happy young adult adventures, but these years would mostly be comprised of sadness and unknown despair.

For my mother, Louisa the news of my grandmother, Linda's illness brought a halt to any educational advancement. My mother, Linda would no longer be afforded the opportunity to pursue an avenue which she desperately wanted to travel. In my mother, Louisa's later years, she would often lament on the insecurity that plagued her due to her lack of education and she would also finally reflect on how lonely her childhood was. How she shared her living quarters with 12 other individuals in her family. Due to lack of space at the dinner table, my mother, Louisa was often confined to sit in the small corner of the room. Although this corner proved to be my mother, Louisa's salvation, it also emphasized the magnitude and depth of her lonely existence. My mother, Louisa would recall on the times when she was a child and sickness befell her, that she was never afforded any sort of tenderness that resembled motherly love. Ultimately, the pain that was brought with the reflection of those moments would abruptly force my mother, to change the subject.

So, after two years spent in the halls of academia, at the age of 16, my mother, being the good daughter dropped out of school and became my grandmother, Linda's primary caretaker. This was the beginning of the role reversal. My mother, Louisa's day consisted of cooking, cleaning, shopping and adhering to the needs and comforts of my grandmother

Louisa and grandfather Marco. Though, a sound of complaint was never uttered publicly from her lips. It was at night, when she approached her sanctuary. It was under the warmth of her covers the she would question both her emotional and physical existence. Also, during this time, of repose, a sense of guilt would rear its ugly head and my mother would ask her maker to forgive her resentfulness and to give her the strength to accept this task gracefully. Eventually, both this and her home employment would continue for a year. My grandmother, Linda's health improved, deciding to take the remission route. With this discovery, my mother, Louisa was able to join the outside world which had been hauntingly beckoning her to rejoin it and be a part of the masses.

Due to the drinking companion who had, since coming to America, established a permanent friendship with my grandfather, Marco, my mother, Louisa was forced to dispel any dreams of pursuing an education. She was needed to help in providing the monetary needs that came with helping to run a household. A friend of the family, aware of her need for employment, found my mother, Louisa a job at a lingerie factory. A job which did not require the prerequisite of having a paper indicating that you occupied space in a four-year institution. But, only having the capability to sew, an ability which she was proficient in due to her economic standing which required that she make her own clothes.

The proceeding next four years consisted of my mother tooling at the lingerie factory. Though not very mind stimulating, it was beneficial in slowly dispelling the shyness and insecurity which encompassed her being. Having a job outside her home enabled her social skills to heighten to a level where she was no longer apprehensive of engaging in social banter. No longer feeling like the little girl crouched in the corner, she found herself bravely sharing her thoughts with coworkers during the hour which they were allotted each day to share meals. It was during this time she developed friendships that would last a lifetime.

It as a Friday afternoon, my mother, journeying home on her usual form of transportation, the bus, it was at this time that was introduced to a young woman through a mutual friend. The young woman named Dina Bergonzi who was also an immigrant and came from the same area of Italy as my mother. This common thread and many others would propel a friendship that entwined their lives forever. They proceeded to converse for the remainder of the ride. Upon reaching her destination, my mother asked her new-found friend where she lived and that she would pay her a visit. To my mother's delight, they were practically neighbors. That evening she told her mother about the new friend she had made on the bus. Her mother, Linda was cautiously optimistic in her response. My grandmother, Linda knew that her daughter's insecurity and overly generous nature was often taken for granted and discarded when her usefulness no longer adhered to their needs. My mother, Louisa continued to argue her case, stating that this time things would be different. My grandmother, Linda silently looked to the sky and prayed for this reality.

The next three years of my mother, Louisa's life consisted of work and developing the friendship which continues to this day. But it was at night, when she reveled in spending quality time with the pots and pans in her tiny kitchen. It was here that her cooking skills reached four-star status. Unfortunately, her secret dream of opening an eating establishment would never see the light of day. My grandmother, Linda's illness refused to remain dormant, my mother's decision to accept the invitation of marriage would permanently dispel and derail any thoughts of fulfilling this dream. Her days would be filled with the duties of a daughter and also a wife. My mother, Louisa was subconsciously tired of bearing the position of chief caretaker, viewed marriage as an opportunity of having someone take care of her.

My mother met the man who would share her life through her best friend, Dina. My mother and my father, Stefano Tiramani also shared the common bond of both being from the same region of Italy. This made the awkwardness of establishing a new relationship much easier. For three years, my mother and father would endeavor to become acquainted with all facets of each other's personality. Upon completion of this adventure, and finding that their two spirits were compatible, they decided that they would travel the adventure of life together. So, on a sunny day in April of 1956, my mother and father sealed the ribbon that would tie their lives together forever. Even though death has separated them, death could not untie the bond that existed between. It remains intact to this day.

My father, Stefano Tiramani, was born in Paris, France on January 19, 1925. On the eve of his second birthday, the family returned to Morfasso, Italy. My father's days consisted of working on the farm. My father, Stefano would get up at 4:30 in the morning and cultivate the farm. My father, Stefano's academic endeavors would not continue beyond the fifth grade. Pursuing his education would force him to commute to a different town. This was not an option for he was needed at home to assist with the farm. At the age of eighteen, he would be called to serve his country. The next two years of his life would be dedicated to fighting the enemy and avoiding being captured. Like many men who served, this subject would never be discussed. Reliving it brought the nightmares back to life. Therefore, this subject would remain taboo.

In 1953, at the age of 28, he would venture to begin a new life in the land of endless opportunity, America. Like most immigrants, he had a sponsor. His sponsor's name was John Oddi. His first residence in this country would be located on 118th Street in Harlem. His first job was working at a restaurant in which his sponsor worked in. Mr. Oddi was a chef at a restaurant called Danny's which was located in the 40's. Mr. Oddi found a job for my father at the restaurant as a bartender. Although, he was eventually offered ownership of the restaurant, being indoors stifled him. The open-air beckoned. Eventually, one of his countrymen who had also come to America would get him into Local

780, which was a union for Cement Masons. Local 780 was primarily comprised of individuals who came from Northern Italy. The president of the union was also from that part of Italy. This work offered him the opportunity to work in the open air. Although the dangerous pitfalls of this profession, any misstep both physically and mentally could potently cause his premature demise, he delighted in the end results of his labor. Knowing that his hands helped in the creation of many of the skyscrapers that grace this city, made it all well worth the toil and sweat.

During the course of my childhood, on various car rides through the city, my father would often proudly point at the various skyscrapers he had a hand in creating. As a child, I often felt as if my father was bragging. Outwardly, I congratulated him but inwardly, embarrassment gripped me. Being humble was a virtue my mother ingrained in me and which I practiced hard to perfect. My father's verbal actions were throwing that thought process out of the window. But I find as the years pass me, I realize that my father was not bragging but this brought him a sense of pride. He was letting me know, that this was who he was and this was whom he wanted me to remember him. My father was correct. This is how his spirit continues to live on. Through the many bricks that compose the many building he so proudly helped to bring to life. As if a walk through the streets of the city, a smile grips the edges of my face, as I do remember.

One of those buildings in which he contributed his talents to, was the World Trade Center. He would have the great honor of working on its Foundation. The horrific events of September 11th washed away any sense of achievement it might have brought in the past. An overwhelming feeling that he might have had a hand in that dispelled any feeling of accomplishment. Future discussion of this horrific event would no longer bring satisfaction but despair in the form of a tear slowly traveling down the wrinkles that would define his later years.

My father, Stefano would often relay many stories about his days on various construction sites. One particular story that comes to mind, particularly because it involves the individual that now occupies the oval office these many years later. As many of you know, Donald Trump's father, Frederick Trump was a prominent real estate developer in New York. My father, Stefano worked on many of Mr. Trump's buildings. My father, Stefano would often relay stories to us on how Frederick Trump would visit the worksites. My father, Stefano always talked about what an amiable man Mr. Frederick Trump was and appreciated his genuine concern for the man who worked on his sites. When Mr. Frederick Trump would visit his sites during the summertime, he would bring along his young son, Donald Trump. Mr. Frederick Trump being acutely aware of the sweltering heat, and its effect on the workers on his sites would ask the younger Donald to give water to each of the men at the site. My father would often say how much this gesture was appreciated and never forgotten.

In his later years, dementia would occupy permanent residency in his head. As is evidenced by many who struggle with this disease, the past is what is remembered. The present is nonexistent. Also, with this specific illness, acceptance is extremely difficult for a person's loved ones. My mother's denial became my forced acceptance. Through the course of his disease, I became both his physical and emotional Guardian. He would finally succumb to kidney failure on June 20, 2012.

My father, though a good man, was human. As I chronically age, I find that I have inherited some of my father's imperfections. Primarily, the great desire to please those around me and my temper erupting when unwarranted. The ladder is something that I have worked most of my life to quell, but sorry to say have been unsuccessful. I am hoping as I progress in my life, eventually with time, I will be able to diminish this trait.

The matriarch of my father's family, my grandfather, Domenico Tiramani was born in June of 1900 in the little town of Morfasso, Italy.

His siblings consisted of two brothers and two sisters. He would never know them. They would leave upon the advent of his birth. On the eve of his second birthday, he would lose his parents. In his later years, when asked about his parents, with a sigh and great sadness would indicate he had no recollection of them. He would be adopted by a neighbor and remained with them for the next sixteen years of life. Upon his sixteenth birthday, he would venture out into the world on his own. He had inherited his parents' home which also included a farm. The farm would provide him with a way of living. He was twenty years old when he married my grandmother, Angela. My grandparents were married for 50 years. My grandmother, Angela would leave this world in 1967 and my grandfather, Domenico would follow on Christmas day in 1973 due to his organs totally shutting down. His son, my father would suffer the same fate.

Out of all the individuals that compromised my family, my grandmother, Angela, remains an enigma. My father's mother, Angela was a ghost like figure in my life. The remaining years of her life were spent in a corner room, not only darkened by closed shades but also by the depression that embraced her being. This would be her existence until she was called to the lord in December 1967.

The beginning of their journey together began at a residence which, according to today's standards, would be considered a very humble abode. A place one would characterize as having the similarities of the quarters which a maid inhabited during the turn of the century. In those days, it was considered a palace. It was located on 105th Street and Third Avenue, not far from my mother's former residence. Unfortunately, it was also at this time that the unwelcomed visitor that had invaded my grandmother's life abruptly reappeared. Her nemesis, cancer, was back. The reappearance of my grandmother's cancer would force both her and my mother to spend the majority of the next three years in and out of hospital rooms.

My mother's early years in her marriage revolved around catering to the needs of others. Her days were spent confined within the stifling four walls of a hospital bedroom playing the part of the dutiful daughter. Her nights were spent adhering to the needs of her husband and the other duties that come with running a household. Many times, during this period she feared that exhaustion would eventually overcome her and permanently inhibit her. It was at these moments that she was grateful adrenalin did not abandon her, but continued to remain the hydration to keep her going. A hydration that would prove vital in enabling her to endure what was to lie ahead. As my grandmother's cancer progressed, it brought with it a life-altering decision. This decision would dictate the many avenues my mother would be forced to take the rest of her life. Ultimately later in her life, it would force her to leave her family for a number of years and ultimately cause uncomfortable lifelong friction.

One fateful day, my grandmother's physician had approached my mother with the news that the cancer had progressed and that my grandmother's leg would need to be amputated. My mother's response was laughter. My mother became alarmingly confused by this uncharacteristic response. It dismayed her to her core, she was taken aback. Her doctor assured her on how the nervous systems responded, very similar crying hysterically. This behavior was often associated with such traumatic instances. instances. As the discussion with her doctor progressed, my mother's defense mechanism in dealing with it was to convince herself that it was just an upcoming pilot for a TV show that would never make to the air. Or, that it was just a bad dream which occurred during her Rem State of sleep and she would wake up from to a day that would have the sun beaming through her window. My grandmother's physician, noting the distant faraway look in my mother's eyes, tried desperately to compassionately ease her fears without dismissing the magnitude of the situation. He wanted her to know, that though the situation would be accompanied with great emotional and decision-making consequences, there is a higher power that will put in place outside forces that will help her through such moments. With this reassurance, my mother was filled with a strong survival mechanism which enabled her to embrace the strong sense that she would get through anything.

Despite my mother's acceptance of my grandmother's fate, she continued to investigate other methods in which to halt the spread of the cancer. After many days filled with much emotional and psychological deliberation and numerous discussions with my grandmother's physician, she realized there was no other solution. Unfortunately, holistic medicine had yet to make an appearance. The secret discussions which my mother engrossed in with a higher power each night, proved to be all for naught and would not be responded to in the way she desired. There would be no angel appearing to impart any divine solution to her situation.

The day of my grandmother's operation had arrived. It was mid-August. My mother was awakened by an unusually strong beam radiating from a warming sun. A beam which systematically propelled my mother to automatically wipe remnants of tears which had found a residence in her eyes during the course of the night. She wearily picked herself up and threw her legs over the side of the bed. She gingerly fell to her knees and beckoned the Lord's assistance in granting her the strength to endure the coming days ahead. Upon completion of her request, she picked herself up and suddenly felt an inner assurance that no matter what lies ahead, she would endure.

She walked into the kitchen and proceeded to make an extremely strong cup of coffee. My father had already left for the day for his job as a laborer. As you will learn, my father did not have the capacity to deal with situations that brought discomfort. As is common with most Italian men of his era, they were usually emotionally retarded to the needs of others. In these situations, they often would bear the resemblance of an uninvited guest, extremely awkward and not wanting to participate in any aspect of this situation. Their main purpose in this whole situation was to make sure their spouses would continue to perform their domestic duties. As the coffee was brewing, my mother proceeded to take a bath and get dressed. She stood before the mirror seeking its approval. The reflection that stood before her was in mother's estimation flawed. Her insecure perception of herself never enabled her to truly accept the reality of what the mirror was actually presenting. Not wanting to elaborate on her reflection, she looked at her watch and realized the time of reckoning was here. She looked for her keys and slammed the door, unaware of her strength. She took a deep breath and ran down the flight of stairs that separated her and the rest of humanity. As her feet touched the hard concrete, the reality of her situation became clearer, and she worked hard to continue to extinguish the tears that desperately tried to escape once again during the light of day. She only allowed herself to cry in the dark of the evening.

My grandmother, Linda and grandfather, Marco resided two blocks away from my mother. My mother was grateful that the short distance afforded her the opportunity for fresh air and a few last quiet moments with her thoughts. As my mother approached the door, she began to knock feverishly. Both her parents greeted her. Her parents, both bore the appearance that sleep had alluded and abandoned them the night before. My mother immediately surmised that this was caused by the worried anticipation that comes with these roadblocks that life tends to occasionally put forth. In her assuring manner, she kissed them and hugged them. My mother, then went into their bedroom to retrieve any items that were needed in assisting them to maneuver any obstacles which this day presented. Upon completion of this task, she gathered her parents into the cab that was waiting for them.

For my mother, the trip to Sloan Kettering felt reminiscent of her first cab ride in her new country. The same feelings of loneliness, fear, despair, which festered in the pit of her stomach were once again resurfacing. She decided to once again, call upon the mind over matter mechanism. As always, she found it to not only be the perfect sedative but also her most ardent supporter.

The day outside mirrored the emotions that were reflected inside, gloomy and matter of fact. As with most cab rides, passengers often feel as if they are somehow sitting on a trampoline. This adventure would be no different, prompting my mother to hold on to the linings of the seat with one hand and with the other to secure her parents. Thankfully, before she could release an additional sigh, they had reached their destination. This destination would not only become a second home for my mother the next two weeks but will also mark the beginning of a long and emotionally arduous journey that would be traveled until my grandmother's last breath.

Upon opening the door, my mother's little family was immediately welcomed by an impersonal, antiseptic environment. This invisible embrace had succeeded in unraveling even further the nerves that continued to wreak havoc with my mother's physical being as opposed to blanketing her with a sea of calm. As they approached the desk, they were received by a compassionate yet serious nurse and given instructions on how they must proceed. My mother often commented that this first encounter would be the sea of calm she had been searching for. It had been neatly disguised as this nurse. A friendship developed between them. This friendship would enable her to endure the two-week aftermath of this difficult episode in her life.

As my grandmother was wheeled into the operating room, the role reversal had commenced with my grandmother clutching my mother's hands. Reminiscent of how, as a child, my mother would often seek comfort in those hands. As she deposited my grandmother in the operating room, my mother would then take the interminable walk to the waiting room where her father embraced her as her dormant emotions finally erupted.

The operation required that my grandmother be under the knife for the majority of the day. The end result would leave her with one visible leg and the other a phantom. Due to the severity of the cut, a prosthesis could never be considered an aid in helping her navigate her everyday life. From that day on, her constant and most trusted companions would be crutches. Upon completion of the operation, my mother and grandfather were instructed by the doctor that they would not be able to see my grandmother that day and to go home and get a good night's sleep. In a gentle yet firm manner, he wanted to prepare them for the bumpy emotional road that lay ahead but also offered a father's encouragement that together they would prevail. Emotionally drained from the earlier events of the day, while on her way home in the taxi, her head immediately tilted to the side and was transported into a deep sleep. A sleep that was only disrupted by her father's booming voice, instructing her that they were home and she needed to wake up. Feeling like an unmovable boulder, she wearily picked herself up and proceeded to pay the cab. Feeling like an unmovable boulder, she wearily picked herself up and proceeded to pay the cab. As she stood in front of her tiny apartment, she wondered if the reservoir of strength and perseverance reserved for such situations, would be sufficient enough to deal with both this and the all too unexpected pregnancy which came to light the week before. It was that moment that she harkened to her mother's advice you do the best you can and take one day at a time. The arduous journey had truly begun.

It all began two weeks after my grandmother's operation. The day after my grandmother returned home from the hospital, my mother's everyday itinerary would be consumed with caring not only for her mother but would also entail the duties required of a married and now pregnant woman. Primarily the house duties, cooking and cleaning and taking care of the needs that come with a pregnancy. My grandfather remained a blimp on the radar. Choosing, like most men, refusing to deal with the situation instead, searching for solace in a bottle of Southern Comfort and handing out random change to the little children to the little children who happily toiled in the streets. Unfortunately, this would be the solution for most of the issues that plagued my grandfather during his life which began after his service in World War I was completed. It became a mainstay in assisting him to squelch the memories and dreams that haunted him due to his military service. In his mind, it worked so well, that through his life, alcohol would be the sedative that would cure all his ills.

My father's main focus during this period was to merely provide the financial assistance that was needed to sustain a family. He did not feel that it was his place to surround my mother with any emotional or physical assistance. Despite all the directions my mother was being pulled, my father still maintained that she continues to adhere to his every need. The old-world Italian mentality of the husband being served and that he was the king of the castle, continued even in a land where this thinking was already taboo. Even going forward, he continued to hark back to the old ways. This is a point which remains a source of contention between family and friends whom he encounters.

My mother's emotional leaning post during this time was my godmother, Dina. She would remain mother's selfless mainstay from that time on. She was the one my mother could go to and verbally release her demons to. My godmother would offer her a cup of coffee that was laced with understanding and a gentle compassionate ear. My godmother, never making any critical judgment in the manner in which my mother dealt with everyday situations. Their conversations mirrored the appearance of a secret therapy session. At the end of each session, my mother's emotional and physical well-being would be replenished to the point that she would be able to conquer any obstacles that her mother's illness would present her each day.

My mother Louisa's unexpected pregnancy, though a blessing, came with the usual residual effects. She was woken each morning by a nausea that came and fortunately for her, quickly passed. She also found her stamina to be in limited quantities. During this time, she often commented on how miraculous it was that she was able to endure and continue during this time. Little did she know, all the emotional ills of this time would surface after the birth of her first child. A deep depression, yet unheard of or named, would befall her.

Even beyond the birth of my brother, Domenic in May of 1957, my godmother remained a mainstay in my mother's life. She continued to assist my mother both physically and emotionally. She would become my brother's second mother and to this day, is still thought of in that manner. A year later, upon the birth of her own child, my brother requested that she immediately return the little person to where he came from. Although her motherly affections towards him never wavered, he resented the division of her attentions. Not wanting my brother to feel as if he had lost a seat in her heart, she continually strived to dispel his second-place insecurities. She even had my brother sit with her while she was feeding, putting to sleep and bathing her son so that he would be acquainted and form easiness and acceptance of his presence in his godmother's life. The great care in which my godmother took in helping to establish a relationship between her son and my brother proved to be extremely successful. They eventually established a relationship that continues to thrive until today.

My godmother continued to care for my brother for two years while my mother played the role of the dutiful daughter, wife and also combating her depression. Upon the completion of the two years, my grandmother and grandfather had become proficient in the management of their plight. It was also at this point, the depression which had possessed my mother both physically and emotionally had released its grip. With these two ingredients in toe, the normality of everyday life had finally returned to my mother and would continue over the next four years in the heart of Harlem.

As the days proceeded by, my parents continued to work vehemently in fattening their bank account. They hoped all the hard work would elevate their station in life. Eventually, it did. They were able to relocate and have their American dream become a reality. Their American dream would be located in the borough of the Bronx in the Pelham Bay Section. This land was purchased in 1694 by Thomas Pell. The neighborhood has proved to be a longstanding dwelling for various peoples who hailed from Italy, Ireland, Greece and Germany. It is only in recent years that there has been an influx of Hispanics. In early 1961, the Pelham Bay Section of the Bronx was still barren and not yet fully developed. At this time, nature still ruled. The majority of the dwellings at that time were scattered and trees occupied most of the landscape. This would all change with the mass exodus of Italian and Irish immigrants from Harlem were seeking their own American Dream like my parents did.

As this dream became a reality, feelings which danced within my parent's soul were composed of excitement, but, and as with unknown endeavors, fear still reared its ugly head. They would, through the course of this difficult transition, be pleasantly surprised by unexpected allies who would lessen the ups and downs of this life-changing direction. These unexpected allies were friends from many areas of the old country who were also migrating to the Bronx. As the years proceeded for all these immigrants, they would find that their close friendships would prove to be the backbone and sturdy encouragement that eased the road to personal success for all of them. They all became each other's emotional leaning posts; always there to check on one another should one of them fall. They held sturdy the ladder of success for each other. Made sure to pick each other up when they fell. I bore witness to this through all my formidable years and this would form my own personal feelings towards the value of close friendships and how vital they are to our existence.

It was at this time, seeing that their daughter was settled, my grandparents, Linda and Marco decided to return to their motherland to live out their remaining years. They ventured back to live their remaining years at the establishment that had now become a thriving bed and breakfast. My grandmother, though limited by her physical impediment, assisted in any manner she could. My grandmother also assisted monetarily by affording them a sum each month with their many expensed.

As you may able to surmise from the personality traits I have written about my father, as far as he was concerned, he was the only one that existed in the world. His needs came first. Though inwardly resentful, my mother, being the dutiful wife complied without complaint. Until his death, this was the blueprint of their marriage. She poured her resentfulness into perfecting her already wonderful skill of cooking. It was during this time that she developed the many wonderful recipes that compelled me to write this book and share it with the rest of the world. Friends and family through various functions often had the great gastronomical pleasure of having their palates stimulated by her mastery. My mother never disappointed. Even now, it saddens me that she never had the encouragement of her partner. If only she was born in a different time and promised to another, I am sure her lifelong dream of owning her own restaurant would have become a reality.

My mother, Louisa was not the only one who experienced a sense of feeling like an indentured servant. I sense, the majority of her peers also traveled this path. The times and their family dictated that they be beholden to their husbands with no regard for their own success. The thought of securing a life outside the confines of their home or seeking any individuality was heresy. This lack of encouragement to find their own path, would eventually bring despair and a world of sadness that engulfed them until they meet their maker. Throughout my youth, this sadness was reflected in my mother's face and continues until this day. Ultimately, her dream of a rustic restaurant introducing the masses to Northern Italian Cuisines would remain, just that, a dream.

◈ *Lynn Tiramani* ◈

My Godmother, Dina: Another Disciple of this Cuisine who influenced me

I have had the great opportunity to be exposed to not one but two wonderful cooks, my mother and my godmother. Despite her contentious relationship with the stove, my godmother's kitchen continued to produce a variety of culinary delights. As I am writing this passage, I am once again transported back in time to a kitchen similar to my mother's. My godmother often defers praise away from herself and onto the cooking virtues of her husband's family. It was in these times that I became acquainted with her mother-in-law. She was reminded of and I was awakened to the magic that her mother-in-law performed in her kitchen.

Unfortunately, my godmother, tragically lost her mother to TB when her mother was 45 and she was just 11. The responsibilities that come with being a wife and mother were then transferred to my godmother. She became a cook, caretaker and housekeeper all at once. She was forced to accept adulthood before she was ready. Although this transition and the climate of war robbed her of any semblance of the activities that come with being a teenager, it did afford her the opportunity to perfect her skills in the kitchen.

As I indicated through my formidable years, the sprouting process was hastened along with the aid of a nightly dinner which consisted of three stages. The welcoming committee which awaited us the table was a bowl of chicken soup. It was common that individuals who migrated from the North began their meal with soup. Their southern counterparts opened each meal with pasta. Although there were many chickens who clamored to be picked, to be the main ingredient in my mother's pot, it was my godmother's edition of this culinary wonder which was often regarded by many to cure common ailments. People often stood in line outside her door for a sample and are now the most requested meal by her grandchildren when they visit. As a young girl,

La Cucina della mia Bisnonna

I thought she had a magic wand that was masquerading as a spoon to stir her soup. Something this wonderful had to be sprinkled with some hidden magic. There was no magic wand, just practice, practice, practice ultimately leading to perfection. In the next paragraph, I would like to give you a glimpse of the foundation that made my godmother into the wonderful cook she is today.

My godmother's mother-in-law, Maria, also called Gropparello her home. Groporello is located 130 kilometers northwest of Bologna and 25 kilometers south of Piacenza. It is estimated to have a population of 2,379. Her mother-in-law was the youngest of three girls. Like my great grandmother, she would suffer the great misfortune of forging through life without her mother. She lost her when she was young.

Upon her mother's death, Maria was adopted by her aunt. It was during the course of her childhood years that her great passion for cooking grew from inquiring about how recipes were made to making them herself. She was given the opportunity to sprout her new-found cooking skills to greater heights. She was required to assist her aunt in the restaurant which she opened in 1910 in their little town called San Michele. San Michele is also in the province of Piacenza. It is minuscule in size and only houses 65 inhabitants.

When the restaurant was initially opened, it was the only restaurant in this little town. It had the capacity to hold 100 patrons. The majority of the patrons were English and French immigrants. It was particularly busy during the summer months. The physical composition of the restaurant was reminiscent of a small medieval castle. All of the food was grown fresh in a garden stationed directly behind the restaurant. The primary beverage of the restaurant was the homemade wine. As with every great cook, she developed all the recipes herself. The most requested of these recipes were her Pasta with Beans and Polenta as well as her Ravioli. The economic climate of the time dictated the cost of the meal. Therefore, whatever a patron could afford was accepted with a gregarious thank you and a smile. Upon her marriage, my godmother's mother-in-law sold the restaurant. Her mother-in-law passed away in 1958, two months before the birth of her first grandson.

Two of Maria's children would continue her legacy of cooking and running a restaurant. Her oldest son, Peter, was given the opportunity to display his cooking skills everyday at the Savoy Hotel. The Savoy Hotel sits on the Strand, which is in the City of Westminster in Central London. The Impresario, Richard Doily Carte, was able to build the hotel through the profits from his Gilbert and Sullivan operas. The hotel opened its doors on August 6, 1889. The Savoy was the first luxury hotel in Britain to have electric lights throughout. The most expensive and lavish rooms contained bathrooms, constant hot and cold water and many of the yet unheard of niceties that we take so much for granted today. The hotel counted among its guest's such notables as George Gershwin, Frank Sinatra, Harry Truman, Judy Garland, Barbara Streisand, the Beatles and many others from the thespian, musical and political realm.

Today, the hotel is managed by Fairmont Hotels and resorts. These days, it has given the title as "London's Most Famous Hotel." To the society which revolves around the hotel and the rest of the world, it is considered one of the most prestigious hotels. It was temporarily closed in December 2007 for extensive renovations and was reopened in October of 2010.

Her oldest daughter, Maria, started her culinary career by being a hostess. Her infectious smile and diligence did not go unnoticed by the owners of the establishment. She was quickly escalated through the ranks and eventually became the manager. This was a monumental achievement in a time when women were still more accepted in the kitchen rather than outside the kitchen. The thought that a woman managed the maneuvers and directions in which a restaurant conducted its business was still rebuffed loudly by the male population in the early

50's. If we look back to that time in our history, society completely restricted the roles of women by expecting them to remain subservient to the needs of their husband. Women were taught, at an early age, that their main goal in life was to be the perfect homemaker and not to stand in front of a boardroom expressing their opinions on how to run a major corporation. Any such thought was considered blasphemous. Therefore, the fact that Maria would soar to such heights was quite a testament to not only her intelligence but also to her unflappable courage despite all odds.

Maria would continue in that position for 22 years. Unfortunately, a weak heart that plagued her since a young age would lead her to a final resting place at the very young age of 57. She passed away two weeks before Christmas in 1977. Although I never had the opportunity to meet Maria, I admire and appreciate her for the way she lived her life. She was truly a maverick and pioneer, and, although gone, her life continues to be an inspiration to all those who came after her.

For the past three years, I have spent the majority of my weekends composing and compiling the various recipes that grace the following pages. These recipes are geared to women who view the kitchen as her second home. This book is definitely not for individuals who cannot conceive turning on the oven. A prerequisite for success with these recipes is having a passion for this form of housework. As with many heirlooms passed down from one generation to the next, this cookbook will eventually develop the appearance of a notebook worn down through the passage of time and transferred from one set of hands to another. It will also become earmarked with various age spots composed of the remnants of tomato sauce, onions, garlic and various treasurers of the culinary world. I know the appearance will give you a glimpse of the warm and comforting feeling of your own mother's kitchen as your travel through the pages of this culinary adventure.

Another reason writing of this book was to pay homage to the many immigrants that grace the shores of this country and their determination to build a better life for themselves and those that would come after. I am sure many of you while reading this book, will be reminded of your own upbringing and give you a greater appreciation of those who went before you the true heroes of our life.

So, I invite you to be my guest and journey with me to the providence of Bologna which is the main culprit in Italy which houses this Northern Italian cuisine. Should you decide to experiment with these recipes, I know, while you are creating and attempting to bring them to life, there you will feel what seems to be an ocean of sweat streaming down your brow. You will also automatically remember to curse in the language of your ancestors. All these feelings are the byproducts of what transpires when you are taking this journey. I am sure upon reaching your destination, the end result will provide raves from all those who are lucky enough to have been invited to partake in the food festivities. I promise their reaction will immediately dispel all of the uncomfortable by-products that accompanied your journey.

Please note that the recipes are not in any order. Some have stories accompanying them. I thought you would be interested in how they came to life. Ultimately, I decided to write this book primary as a way of paying homage to the wonderful cooks who have graced my life and whose legacy of cooking will continue to live on through the generations that precede them.

I hope you enjoy this book which I hope will grace your coffee table for many years to come and hopefully makes you think of the cooks that have come before you.

My Godmother's Famous Chicken Soup

RECIPE

INGREDIENTS

Chicken (5 Legs)
Beef (3 Pounds)
Carrot (1 Small)
Water (5 Quarts)
Garlic (2 Pieces)
Onion (½)
Leeks (2 Small Leeks)
Celery (1 Stalk)
Tomato (½ a Medium One)
Bouillon Cubes (1 Chicken And 1 Beef)
Parsley (A Tablespoon)
Salt (4 Tablespoons)
Pepper (1 Tablespoon)

UTENSILS

Pot (One Big Pot)
Bowels (Thee Big)
Strainer (Medium Size)
Spoon (One Big Spoon)

Begin by taking you big pot to the sink. Take your five pieces of chicken and three pounds of beef assemble them in your pot then fill it up with water leaving an inch from the top. Add your five tablespoons of salt, a teaspoon of pepper, parsley and your two bouillon cubes. Bring your pot to the stove. Let your soup boil profusely on high heat for fifteen minutes. While the soup is cooking, a film will develop. You will need to strain that from the soup. After you have strained all the film, you would add your carrot, garlic, small leeks, tomato, parsley, celery and onions. You would let your soup slow boil over medium to low heat for about two and a half hours. During the cooking process continue to taste to see if additional salt is needed. Also, during the cooking process, please continue to stir your soup to make sure that the meat and the other ingredients, do not stick to the bottom of the pot.

After your soup has completed cooking, you would remove your pot from the stove and bring it over to your sink. Take your three big round bowels and your strainer. Slowly pour the contents through the strainer right into the bowel. Continue this procedure until all the contents of your pot have been emptied in your bowels. This recipe should give you enough for three bowls. Put your bowels on the side to let cool. After they have cooled put in the refrigerator. This soup will last for a week.

Here is a tip on what to do with the leftover chicken. You would chop it up and season it will oil and salt.

The Two Ladies Spinach Soup

RECIPE

INGREDIENTS

Fresh Spinach (2 Cups)
Bouillon Chicken (1 Cube)
Water (To Fill Pot And Boil)
Oil (Enough To Cover Bottom Of Pot)
Soup (1 ½ a Cup)
Salt (1 Tablespoon)

UTENSILS

Pots (Two Medium Sized)
Grater (One Medium Size)
Strainer (One Medium Size)
Bowl (Large Bowl)
Pot (One Small Sized)

Take your medium pot and add your water, tablespoon of salt and your spinach. Let your spinach cook for about seven minutes or to your taste. While your spinach is cooking, take your small pot to add your water and soup. Let your water and soup simmer to a boil. You will need to add it to your spinach later on. When your spinach is cooked, strain it. Let it cool. When it has sufficiently cooled, you would finely chop your spinach. Take your medium pot with your heat on high; add oil enough to cover the bottom and your chicken bouillon cube. Make sure your chicken bouillon cube melts. This should take about five minutes. With your heat still on high add your chopped spinach. Stir your spinach for about ten minutes. You would then take the water and soup that was boiling in your small pot and add it to the spinach. Let your spinach and water boil on high heat for about 15 minutes. After the 15 minutes, you would add your pasta or your rice. Your rice should cook approximately 20 minutes. Your pasta should cook about 11 minutes. Bring to the table and serve in soup boils. As an aside, if you would like, you may add parmesan cheese.

Minestrone (Italian Vegetable Soup)

RECIPE

INGREDIENTS

Parsley (3 Teaspoons)

Celery - (3 Stalks)

Pepper - (1 Pinch)

Rosemary - (1 ½ Teaspoon)

Garlic - (3 Cloves Of Garlic Chopped)

Chicken Bouillon (1 Cube)

Oil – (Enough To Cover Pot)

Beans – (½ Cup To Be Soaked)

Lentils – (½ Cup)

Beef (1 Piece)

Chicken (4 Legs)

Elbow Macaroni (½ cup)

Salt (1 Tablespoon)

UTENSILS

Big Bowls (Two Bowls)

Pot (One Medium Sized)

Pot (One Big Pot)

Strainer (One Medium Size)

You would begin this recipe the day before by soaking your beans overnight. This will soften the beans and enable them to cook faster. The lentils and split peas do not need to be soaked. Take your big pot and fill it with water add your tablespoon of salt. Have the water simmer to a boil. While you are waiting for your water to boil, chop your garlic, parsley, celery, and rosemary you would also add a dash of pepper in the mix. Take your small pot and cover the base of your pot with olive oil. Take your medium-sized pot to add your parsley, celery, pepper, rosemary, chopped garlic, and chicken bouillon cube. On high heat, you would sauté these ingredients for about 15 minutes. After sautéing for 15 minutes, add your lentils, beans, split peas, piece of beef and chicken legs. Leaving your heat on high, stir all these ingredients for an additional 15 minutes. Then lower your heat. By this time, the water that is in your other pot has been brought to a boil. You would take all your sautéed ingredients and add it to the boiled water. This should cook from one and a half hour to two hours. After the soup is cooked, you would then strain all your ingredients. This should make about two bowls of soup. When you decide to have the soup as a meal, you would place your soup in a pot and bring it to a boil and add your pasta. The best pasta to use for this is elbows.

Burdetto (Soup with Eggs)

Unlike the other soups, I have a story for how this soup came to be. As a child, this is one of my mother's soups that I often made a personal request for a day ahead to make sure my mother would make it. More times than not, prior to my request, I would rummage through the kitchen to make sure the ingredients were available. If not, I would get my mother's pocketbook and physically position her towards the supermarket. As a caring mother, she would be happy to accommodate my cravings. I believe after your family has sampled this soup; you too will be happy to accommodate your family's likely continued requests for it.

My godmother often told the story of her brother-in-law, who as you know, was a chief himself. Had a great affection for this peasant fare. He would often say to those who would listen, that he preferred this soup above any other Italian aristocratic fare. He often argued with his peers that this was the manna from God and not ravioli. Trust me, this statement brought him confused, apprehensive stares from the hierarchy of the Italian masses, but the common folk would often nod in approval.

Folklore has it that this recipe was conceived many years ago as a remedy to combat the common cold. Taking a cue from their forefathers that natural remedies were the key to ultimate health, my ancestors used food as a cure for most common ailments. Also, their economic situation and the times warranted them from affording pharmaceutical cures. This soup would prove to be one of the most soothing concoctions that made the ills of a common cold manageable.

Lynn Tiramani

RECIPE

INGREDIENTS

Eggs (3 Eggs To Be Beaten)

Pepper (A Pinch)

Nutmeg (A Pinch)

Parmesan Cheese (3 Tablespoons)

Godmother's Chicken Soup
(1 Medium Size Pot)

UTENSILS

Pot (Medium Size)

Fork (One Regular Size)

Take my godmother's chicken soup and bring it to a boil. While your soup is boiling, you would prepare your mixture. Take your three eggs, pepper and parmesan cheese and beat them thoroughly. When your soup has come to a boil, you would increase your heat and add your mixture. Stir this mixture into your soup until it thickens. This would take approximately ten minutes. When the mixture has thickened, it is ready.

When serving in soup bowls, add a pinch of nutmeg.

Pasta with Beans (Fagoli)

RECIPE

INGREDIENTS

Beans (1 Cup Of Beans Soaked)
Onion (2 Chopped Onions)
Celery (1 stick)
Garlic (3 Cloves Chopped)
Parsley (1 Tablespoon Chopped)
Leek (½ of a Stalk Chopped)
Soup (1 Small Pot Or Medium Size)
Depends on how much you make
Tomato Paste (2 Tablespoons)
Chicken Legs (2 Legs)
Pasta (1 Cup and ½) The tubular type or various small pasta's

UTENSILS

Pot (One Small)
Pot (Medium Size)
Soup (One Big)

Chop your onions, garlic, parsley and leek. Cover the bottom of your bottom with oil. Place all your ingredients in a pot. Let your ingredients sauté on high heat for fifteen minutes. Then lower your flame and cover your pot and let your ingredients cook for approximately 45 minutes to an hour. While these ingredients are cooking, on the side, have my godmother's chicken soup being brought to a boil. When the soup has been brought to a boil, you would add two tablespoons of tomato paste and make sure you dissolve the tomato paste. You will add the soup and tomato paste to you other ingredients later. When your onions, garlic and parsley are totally cooked and developed a pureed constancy, turn the heat on high and add your beans and chicken legs. Sautee the beans and chicken legs on high heat for about three to five minutes. After it has been sautéed for three to five minutes, add the boiling soup.

IMPORTANT NOTE

If you are using dry beans, have them soak in water overnight. The dry beans would then cook in your soup for about an hour to an hour and a half. If you are using fresh, they just need to be cooked for a half an hour to an hour.

Now, you would take your second pot to add your water and tablespoon of salt. Have your water simmer, bringing it to a boil. When your water has been brought to a boil, add your pasta. Let it cook for about 7 to 11 minutes. When the pasta is cooked combine it with your beans. You would then add some of your pasta water to the beans and pasta. You do this, you want your dish to have a bit of a wet consistency or else it will be too dry. But, remember, just a little. You do not want it too soupy. Using a small shaped pasta would be best. This is because you want to be able to have both the pasta and the beans fit on the spoon together. You want to get the full effect of both flavors.

Louisa's Marinara Sauce

As I compose this next recipe, I find myself suddenly transported in time, back to my mother's kitchen in the Bronx. Though the space was very compact, it was big enough to hold all the needed cooking wands to create culinary magic. As I recall this special time, I am filled with not so fond and shaking head memories of my first times trying to make this sauce and trying to duplicate my mother's very proficient cooking skills. Though in the beginning, numerous times wildly unsuccessful, I finally mastered it. I cringe as I recall my first attempts. The end result had the appearance of dark red water with an overly sweet taste. The overly sweet taste was my exaggerated fear that the acid that is the main component in the tomato sauce would overpower the wonderful taste that would be my mother's marina sauce. Hence, my sauce would be a dark, red sweet water concoction that after tasting would find its final resting place down my mother's sink.

My mother, seeing my frustration and dismay would always remind me that her first attempts also garnered the same results. Always reassuring me, that I if I did not give up, I would eventually get it right. Deep down, my mother knew, that despite my great frustration, I would forge on. I am happy to say that I did heed her advice and eventually mastered the sauce. Though, I might add never as good as my mother.

As I reflect on this time, I realize this particular moment enhanced my life in two ways. Not only did I master the sauce, but during this process, a miracle occurred. That miracle, being a kind sentiment actually muttered from the lips of my mother. A woman who was unable to express such emotion. An emotion, which as I chronologically progressed in my life, would never be uttered again and remain forever frozen in time.

In my younger days, I was unable to comprehend as to what caused her to treat me in this manner. But as I grew older and began to understand the psychology which propelled her to respond to me in this manner was taught to her by her own mother. My grandmother's way to deal with my mother's existence was the same response she had towards me. The result was an unwarranted and uncompromising heirloom which was handed down very successfully from one generation to another. In my later years, I confronted my mother regarding this. After much emotional discussion, I came to understand and in turn forgave her. My forgiveness would ultimately be the final solution to this unwanted chapter in my life. Tough the year and practice have made her more proficient in the encouragement department; she still has not perfected the concept. Still, this final solution has enabled both of us to be understanding and compassionate towards each other's shortcomings.

As I introduce you to this next recipe, I think of how my mother would often say that took more than a few tries to perfect this recipe. Those first times, her sauce lacked thickness. Many people use cornstarch to achieve thickness. Through years of experimentation, she realized making the water boil on high heat for a period of time, would achieve the thickness. Through the years, this sauce continues to accompany many of her recipes and bring them to greater tasting gastronomical heights.

My mother often combines this sauce with her porcini sauce. She uses this combined sauce for her lasagna, chicken parmigiana, eggplant parmigiana and ravioli. You will find the recipe later in this chapter.

La Cucina della mia Bisnonna

RECIPE

INGREDIENTS

Celery (2 Stalks Chopped)
Garlic (3 or 4 Cloves Chopped)
Chicken Bouillon Cube (½ A Large)
Leek (1 Stalk Chopped)
Oil (3 Tablespoons)
Oregano (A Pinch)
Basil (A Pinch)
Parsley (A Pinch)
Rosemary (A pinch)
Sugar (1 Teaspoon)
Tomato Sauce (3 Cups)
Salt (½ Teaspoon)
Pepper (A Pinch)
Tomato Paste (1 Tablespoon)
Chicken Stock (1 Cup)
Water (1 Cup)

UTENSILS

Pot (One Big Pot)
Small Pot (Two)
Large Spoon (One)

Chop together your celery, garlic and leek. Take your big pot to add your oil enough to cover the base of your pot and your bouillon cube. On high heat, add all your chopped ingredients, Sautee' your ingredients for about five minutes. Continuing to keep your heat on high for an additional five minutes, add your oregano, basil, parsley and rosemary. Then lower your heat and have these ingredients cook thoroughly for about 30 minutes. While this is cooking, have your water or your soup simmering in your small pot bringing it to a boil. After your ingredients have cooked thoroughly, you would once again put your heat on high and add your tablespoon of tomato paste. Stir with the other ingredients for about five minutes. After the five minutes, continue to keep the heat on high and add your tomato sauce either from a (store brand or the recipe in this book) and your teaspoon of sugar. The sugar will cut the acidity of the tomato sauce. You would then let it boil feverishly for about ten minutes. This will thicken the sauce as opposed to using corn starch. After the ten minutes, you would add the chicken soup or water that has been boiling on the side. As the sauce is cooking, you would continue to add the tomato sauce and soup or water at intervals. Always remember each time you add the tomato sauce or water you should raise your heat for five minutes. After you have finished adding your tomato sauce or water, you would lower your heat and cover the sauce. There should be a little space between the edge of the pot and the cover. This also helps to thicken the sauce. Let your sauce simmer for about 45 minutes to an hour.

Homemade Tomato Sauce for Sauce

As a child, I often wondered why my mother's tomato sauce always had an earthier and fresher taste than the ones I had in restaurants. One Saturday morning, many years ago, I think I was about fourteen at the time; I woke up rubbing my bleary eyes. The remnants of watching TV way passed my normal bedtime. It was Friday after all! Although my eyes may not have been ready to be awakened by the light of day, my nose was pleasantly awakened by the smell emanating from the kitchen. The culprit- my mother's homemade tomato sauce. She had risen early purposely to make a few pots so that she would be able to store them for the winter. This would serve as the main ingredient for her Marinara Sauce. This main ingredient would continue to pleasantly awaken my nose.

RECIPE

INGREDIENTS

Tomatoes (6 cut up)
Sugar (1 Tablespoon)
Chicken Bouillon Cube (1)
Basil (A pinch)
Oil (Enough to cover pan)
Garlic (2 Gloves chopped)

UTENSILS

A Strainer (One Medium Size)
Small Pot (One)
Medium Pot (One)
Medium Spoon (One)

Cut up your six tomatoes. Put them in your small pot. Turn your heat on high, stir and have them reduce because you will strain them. When your tomatoes are reduced, you would put them in your strainer. Take your spoon and mash your tomatoes to release as much of the liquid out of the tomatoes as possible. Take your medium pot, putting your heat on high. Always remember to add enough oil to cover the bottom of the pot and your bouillon cube and your strained tomatoes. After adding the strained tomatoes, your heat should remain on high for about five minutes. After about five minutes, add your sugar parsley and basil to taste. Lower your heat and then let it continue to cook on a slow boil for an additional a half hour.

Nonna's Sweet and Sour Sauce

This next recipe is the perfect culinary potion to enhance even the most mundane or lifeless food. It was concocted on a whim. My mother felt there were some foods in her repertoire that needed fine-tuning. One, in particular, was the always dry and nondescript chicken breast. Also, included in that category are the old reliable standby chicken and veal cutlets. These foods primarily serve as the understudies in the kitchen when the main course cannot be decided on or when a supermarket visit has been deterred for reason beyond the cook's control. My mother tiring, of the uninspired and bland performance of these understudies, decided it was time to spruce them up a bit.

My mother and I would often spend days convened in the kitchen putting on our Einstein hats hoping he would shine some intellectual, chemical intervention that would form the perfect marriage of flavors. Unfortunately, the many mainstays which we called upon, never quite clicked. Opposites do not attract when establishing a permanent relationship of flavors. Though often deterred, we vowed to continue our quest in finding the perfect sauce to make these foods sing with flavor.

Through the years, my mother continued in her desperate quest in searching for the perfect accompaniment to this mundane food. Unfortunately, the word baffled continued to rein from her lips. Not one to give up, she sought the autumn air for inspiration. There was always something in the fall air that seemed to awaken her senses. It was the stirring leaves that rustled against my mother's window pane that seem to subconsciously harass and stimulate the dormant recipe development section of her brain. The constant rattling spewed out the following recipe. A recipe which had her using every viable ingredient. A prerequisite of this recipe is that you will need to devote a day of your life to it. Trust me, it is worth the labor.

So on an autumn day in 2010, she stood in front of the cabinets and the refrigerator that contained the various parts of this potion, her culinary light brightened with blind force in her head. How about a sauce which possessed a sweet and sour component? The Chinese influence that had been hidden in her head finally came out from behind the shadows. With that said, her hands automatically began to pull out the various items throughout the kitchen. She first went to the refrigerator to get her always reliable and mainstay ingredients such as leek, celery and parsley. She then detoured to the meat section and pulled out various pieces of meat which need to be clinging to a bone for the full effect. This was the sour effect. She then proceeded to the fruit section of the kitchen. She found that dried plums, orange peels and two Bosco pears would do nicely. She was set, and now I am set to introduce you to this intense recipe. As the years went on, she would further enhance the recipe by adding other dried fruits such as dried cranberries and dried prunes.

I am calling this Nonna's Sweet and Sour Sauce because it is my Niece's favorite sauce of many which her Nonna makes. She always makes a special request for it. Particularly at Thanksgiving time. It has proven to be a wonderful complement to the turkey. Although a great deal of work, no Italian Grandmother refuses her grandchild.

◦◦◦ *La Cucina della mia Bisnonna* ◦◦◦

RECIPE

INGREDIENTS

Blackberry Brandy (½ Cup)

Leeks (3 stalks)

Celery (4 stalks)

Meat with bones (Veal, Pork, Chicken Whatever you have)

Dried Plums (1 cup)

Orange Peels (The Peels from 2 Large Oranges)

Olive Oil to cover pan (5 Tablespoons)

Handful of Porcini Mushrooms (Dried Do Not Soak)

Dried Cranberries (1 cup)

Dried Prunes (1 cup)

Bullion Cube (1)

Bosc Pears (2)

UTENSILS

Big Pot (One)

Medium Pot (One)

Strainer (One Big)

Big Spoon (One)

Chop your leeks and celery. Take your medium pot and cover the base of the pot with olive oil and add your bouillon cube. Add the chopped leeks, celery, dried plums, orange peels, dried cranberries, dried prunes, Bosco pears and your various meats. Turn your heat on high and sauté these ingredients for about ten minutes. Then you would cover your pot and lower your heat and let cook for three hours. About a half hour before those ingredients have completed cooking, take the big pot that you have on the side and fill it with water. Your water must simmer and be brought to a boil. When the water has been brought to the boil add your ingredients that have completed cooking for three hours and add your porcini mushrooms and ½ cup of Blackberry Brandy. You will continue cooking this for an additional one hour. This will fill one medium-sized container. Just put it in the freezer door and use when needed.

Besides being a wonderful sauce for chicken and veal cutlets, it may also serve as a gray to complement your Thanksgiving Turkey.

Porcini Mushroom Sauce

When the 6, 000 Northern Italians stepped foot on this land they brought with them a very special gift from the motherland. A gift, which would ultimately be treasured and appreciated by many generations to follow. This gift is their Nonna's Porcini Tomato Sauce. What a surprise!! Certainly not a gift in the vain Michelangelo David or the Sistine chapel but food. This sauce would eventually be handed down from one generation to the next. My niece would often say, "Nonna, you could shower your sauce on an old pair of shoes and they would even taste good." Through the years, I would come to find, that my mother must have made the greatest version of this sauce. Because before long, despite trying to keep her version as secretive as an old family recipe, word spread throughout the little corner of the world called the Bronx. Some of the children of my mother's friends would often pester their mother to make a special request to their friend, Louisa for her sauce. In fact, one of my mother's friends said that her daughter bribed her. She promised to make curfew in order to obtain this precious potion. My mother, often embarrassed by this, would work vehemently to convince these youngsters that their mother's sauce was just as good or even better. She often felt like a member of congress, no matter how much she filibustered regarding the attributes of their own mother's sauce, they were not convinced. Finally, through much deliberation my mother would shyly adhere to their wishes and eventually provide them with jars of this treasure.

The ingredient that gives this recipe its unforgettable flavor are the porcini mushrooms. Let me give you some insight into what makes this precious jewel of the mushroom family. The best way to describe the makeup of porcini mushroom is that they have a chewy texture and a taste that bears a very strong earthy, nutty-woodsy, sweet and meaty taste. They have a rich brown color with tinges of yellow. Porcini's are very popular in Italian cooking. My mother and many of her Italian friends would use them in risotto, pasta, sauces, soups, casseroles, and stuffing.

When bought in America, they are exceedingly expensive. Knowing there is an overabundance in their homeland, when a friend or relative went to Italy, they would often bring back this treasure in great quantity for all to share. Due to the porcini's prominent flavor, only a small quantity is any recipe that you use it for. The quantity usually lasted until another friend or relative ventured to Italy it is at this point that the supply would be replenished.

Today, I use the porcini mushroom in many of the recipes inherited from my mother's kitchen. Through the years, I have come to even more appreciate the wonderful flavor of the porcini mushroom.

RECIPE

INGREDIENTS

Onions (3 Medium)

Garlic cloves (3 pieces)

Celery (1 stalk)

Leeks (5 pieces)

Tomato Paste (1 Tablespoon)

Tomato sauce (Canned or you own, 2 Cups)

Chicken Bouillon Cube (1 piece)

Porcini Mushrooms (½ cup)

Butter (1 pat)

Olive oil (Enough to cover the pan)

Water (Enough to fill a pot)

UTENSILS

Pot (Large)

Small Pots (Two)

Big Spoon (One)

Take your ½ cup of porcini mushrooms and place them in water. They will need to be finely chopped prior to adding them to your recipe so they need to be softened. You would then chop your onions, garlic, celery and leek. Take your large pot, cover the base with olive oil, a pat of butter and your bouillon cube. Add your chopped ingredients to your pot with your heat on high. Stir your ingredients for about five minutes. Then, lower the heat. Place your cover on the pot this will cook for about 45 minutes to an hour. Always remember, your ingredients must be thoroughly cooked. While these ingredients are cooking, in two other separate pots, you should have your water and in the other pot your tomato sauce. Having them both simmer and then brought to a boil. When your onions and other ingredients have completed cooking, you would raise your heat and stir in your finely chopped porcini mushrooms. After five minutes of stirring your mushrooms and having the heat on high, you would then add the water from the mushrooms. Let the mushroom water boil ferociously for about 10 minutes. Then with the heat still on high, add and stir in your two tablespoons of tomato paste. After the 10 minutes of letting the tomato paste dissolved in the water, stir in your tomato sauce let it boil continuing to leave the heat on high for about five minutes. You would then add the water that has boiled, and let this continue to boil feverishly on high for about 10 minutes. You will continue to alternate adding the water and tomato sauce. When you alternating these two ingredients, wait at least five minutes each time before adding another ladle. After you have emptied both your pots that contained the water and sauce, lower your heat. Let your sauces cook for an extra 45 minutes to an hour. Do not fully cover your pot. As always, leave a little space between the rim of the pot and your cover.

Garlic and Oil Sauce

During the course of my life, there is one recipe that my taste buds have always had a great affection for. This is pasta dressed with garlic and oil. Unfortunately, many of the restaurants which offer this fair, generally drown the pasta in the oil, leaving the diner feeling like they ingested a bowl of oil with the remnants of limp pasta clinging to the bottom. Unfortunately, garlic often considered an afterthought, the forgotten child in the room. These restaurant facsimiles make me run, not walk back to my mother's humble kitchen for the real thing.

Like me, my mother was often disappointed with the oil and garlic pasta dishes that were often presented to her at various functions. Like most Italians of her generation, they very rarely embarked on an adventure to a local restaurant. Such a trip only occurred on mandatory special occasions or the annual Italian dance. This being one of the characteristics of my upbringing, it was only in my later, formidable years that I had the opportunity to venture to various eateries. But when the occasion called for her to have dinner at another destination and the menu called for a garlic and oil pasta, she was often disappointed. She was disappointed with the artistry of the chef, vehemently indicating how there was no thought process in the making of the dish. She would say that anyone who held the title of chef should have the ability to make the simplest dishes fit for a king.

Not one to be dissuaded by a cooking challenge, through years of experimentation, my mother finally developed the ultimate version of this recipe. A recipe whose ingredients, you will find, magnificently end up hugging your pasta and will make your taste buds sing. I promise, it will enable you to dispel all the bad memories of the oil-soaked concoctions which you were probably presented with in the past. Although you will find it to be more labor-intensive, it is definitely worth the time.

RECIPE

INGREDIENTS

Cloves of Garlic (6 Cloves)

Stalks of Celery (2 Stalks)

Leeks (1 Stalk)

Oil (Enough to Cover Bottom of Pan)

Cube (1 Of Either Chicken or Beef)

Chicken Soup (2 cups)

Half Box (Fettucine or Spaghetti)

UTENSILS

Deep Frying Pan (One)

Pot (Small to Medium)

Chop your leek, celery and garlic. Cover the bottom of the pot with your olive oil. Add your bouillon cube and your chopped ingredients. Let these ingredients cook for thirty minutes. While these are cooking, in your medium pot have your soup simmering bringing it to a boil. When your chopped ingredients have finished cooking, turn your heat on high and add your soup. Let this boil feverishly for about five minutes. You would then lower your heat, put your cover on and let your sauce simmer on low heat for about 30 minutes. When serving this with your pasta, you would take either your spaghetti or linguine, whatever pasta you chose, and pour it directly in your saucepan and stir.

Tripe

This recipe is my grandmother's recipe. As you know, this recipe is the lining of the stomach of a cow. People who were never introduced to tripe, and for the first time hear what it is, quickly reacted like a child who was pushing away their vegetables. They don't want any part of it. But I promise, after you have a taste of this, you will want to revisit this recipe at least once a month. Believe it or not, this was the perfect cure for depression. My godmother would often give this to individual show were feeling blue. After one taste, the skies truly brightened.

RECIPE

INGREDIENTS

Tripe (2 Pounds)
Onions (2 Large)
Garlic (2 Cloves)
Celery (2 Stalks)
Rosemary (1 Pinch)
White wine (1 Glass of White Wine)
Salt (2 Tablespoons)
Tomato Paste (Generally 2 Tablespoons But, Use Your Judgment)
Parsley (2 Tablespoons)
Chicken Stock (Enough to Fill A Small Pot)
Pepper (1 Teaspoon)
Bouillon Cube (1)

UTENSILS

Pot (1 Large Pot)
Pot (1 Small for Soup)

Take your two pounds of tripe and cut into spaghetti strips. Wash it and boil it in glass of white wine, water and two tablespoons of salt for about ten minutes. Take your onions, garlic, celery, and rosemary and chop them thoroughly. Take your large pan and coat with oil and one bouillon cube. Take your chopped ingredients stir on high heat for ten minutes. Lower your heat and then cook for an hour stirring occasionally. After your chopped ingredients have cooked, turn your heat on high and add your tripe and your parsley. Keep the heat on high for about five minutes and stir the ingredients. Leave some parsley aside, you will add this to the tripe as garnish when you are ready to serve it. Lower your heat. You would let your tripe cook for about a two and a half to three hours. At the half-hour point, put your heat on high and add your two tablespoons of tomato paste and stir it in until dissolved. You would then continue to keep on high add a ladle of chicken soup. Continue to keep your heat on high for ten minutes. Then lower your heat. As the tripe is cooking, continue to add your ladle of soup until it is finished. Remember to always increase your heat for five minutes each time you add a ladle of soup. Also remember, white the tripe is cooking, continue to taste to see if you need to add extra salt or pepper. Make sure your pot is totally covered during the cooking process and is simmering on low heat. Should you find your sauce becoming too thick, please leave a little space from your cover and edge of pot. When your tripe has completed cooking, serve in a platter and sprinkle on your leftover parsley.

Chicken Cacciatori

As with all great cooks, they have one signature dish which truly stamps their validity in the great cooks' universe. For my mother, it is her chicken Cacciatori. This is the number one requested recipe in my mother's bad of culinary wonders among her friends. My mother found that this food was the perfect partner for the ultimate Italian pheasant food, Polenta. A combination which would not only warm you during a long winter's day but also has proven to be the perfect sedative for the screaming calls of your rumbling stomach. When you are done enjoying this wonderful concoction, you may feel the need to release your belt an additional notch.

My nephew, though enamored with the various dishes of my mother's kitchen, preferred this dish above all. During the intervals that required him to be home during his college career, she would often welcome him with a dish of polenta accompanied by her famous chicken Cacciatori. He would often be filled with despair when he was had to return to school, knowing it would be some time before his stomach would once again welcome such fare. The main ingredients of this recipe vary throughout the regions of Italy. The majority of these recipes has one particular ingredient in common, is peppers. My mother's recipe could almost be viewed as rebellious. It dispenses any use of pepper in her version of this recipe. But instead prefers to call on her no-miss trustworthy old reliables such garlic, onions and porcini mushroom. As most true cooks know, different versions of a recipe do not cause an uprising or jealousy in the true cooking community but instead, is appreciated and praised for its innovativeness.

La Cucina della mia Bisnonna

As I indicated, this is my Mom's recipes which is worthy of a four-star rating. After you have combined these wonderful flavors and completed the cooking process, you will have even the toughest critics coming back for seconds. Just wait and see.

RECIPE

INGREDIENTS

Chicken (1 Package of Thighs)

Onions (2 Large and 3 Small)

Rosemary (Fresh, if not use dry) Put to Taste

Tomato paste (1 Tablespoon)

Five Porcini mushrooms (Soak in Water)

Chicken Soup or Water (½ a Cup)

Oil (5 Tablespoons or Enough To Cover Base Of Pot)

Butter (1 Pat of Butter)

Bouillon Cube (1 Chicken Cube)

Garlic (3 Gloves Chopped)

UTENSILS

Large Pot (One)

Medium Pot (One)

Spoon (One)

Take your porcini mushrooms and put them in a glass of water. You do that because you need the mushrooms to soften. When they have softened, chop them. You would then take your medium pot and add your water or soup and have it simmer to a boil. While your soup or water is simmering, chop your onions, garlic and rosemary. After you have finished chopping your onions and garlic, take your big pot and add your oil, enough to cover the base of your pot, pat of butter your chopped ingredients. With your heat on high stir your ingredients for about five minutes. Then you would lower your heat and proceed to let your chopped ingredients cook for about 45 minutes. After they are cooked thoroughly, you would then put your heat on high and add your chicken. Stir your chicken for about five minutes. continuing to keep the heat on high for an additional five minutes, add your mushrooms, tomato paste and water or soup to the chicken. After stirring five minutes, you would lower your heat and proceed to let the chicken cook for about an hour. Make sure when you are cooking the chicken, you would leave a little space between the edge of the lid and the pot. This will enable the sauce to get thick. If you find it getting too thick, just take off the cover. Know that while your chicken is cooking, your water and soup will absorb. As it absorbs each time, continue to add your water and soup that you boiled in the pot until it is finished. Each time you add water and soup, make sure your heat is on high for about five minutes, then lower it. After you have completed this pot of water, you would then add the water leftover from the glass your porcini mushrooms were soaking in.

Polenta

In my mother's town and all the towns surrounding her, Polenta was held with great reverence primarily because it rescued the pheasants from ever entering the purgatory of starvation. Polenta would prove to be a substantial mania which filled their bellies, adequately enough to assist them in accomplishing their tasks at hand.

The lands of Northern Italy are known to be the most fertile in Italy. This land would prove to be the perfect landscape to harvest the corn for this potent food energizer. It is initially planted during the spring. By the time September comes around, it is ready to be harvested.

During the course of my childhood, in our small kitchen in the Bronx, I often had the great pleasure of observing my mother and Godmother cook the polenta. I found myself marveling at the stamina my mother and godmother displayed in stirring the cornmeal. pot. A stamina built up during the course of many years of practice. Even more amazing was the utensil they used which is a stick that looks like a shepherd's staff. The main tool in creating this was the pot. The big cast iron pot they used to cook it in, like my mother and godmother, bears all the scars and residue of all the generations of their family that came before them. As a child, I would often wiggle in between and beg that they let me stir the polenta. They would often caution me of the difficulty but I was relentless in my pursuit. Finally, they gave in and adhered to my wishes. I realized, after one stir, I felt like I was stirring dry concrete. I then immediately passed the baton back to my mother. Her look of I told you so, shined more brightly than words can express. As an adult, looking back, I think the fervor in which they attacked the polenta enabled them to dispel all the demons of their war-scarred childhood. This emotional release enabled them to establish the perfect texture for the polenta.

RECIPE

INGREDIENTS	**UTENSILS**
Cornmeal (1 Bag of Goya)	Big Pot (One)
Potatoes (Depends How Big the Pot)	Medium Pot (One)
Water (Filled Pot)	A Big Stirrer
Sauce (1 Small Pot)	Ladle (One)
Cheese (1 Dish of Cheese)	Large Platter (One)
(Either parmesan or Munster)	
Top of Polenta	

Fill your pot with water and a tablespoon of salt, add your potatoes. Cook your potatoes for about an hour. When they are completely cooked, mash them. Please keep the water that you cooked the potatoes in. The water will be a vital component in cooking the polenta. In the other pot, combine the polenta and the mashed potatoes and cook on medium heat. While cooking the polenta, you would keep stirring it, adding the water that you cooked the potatoes in. As the water absorbs, continue you to add a ladle of water. Polenta generally takes about 45 minutes to cook. If the polenta has cooked correctly, it usually obtains a dense texture. When it is ready take your pot of polenta and turn it over. It should resemble a big cake. This will enable you to cut it like into cake slices. Place it on your plate and on top, add a slice of cheese and sauce. The best type of cheese to use is Munster cheese. When served hot, the cheese will melt gloriously over the polenta. Truly food fit for a king.

When you do not have the luxury of having a new dish each day due to the turbulent economic times in a land occupied by unwanted guns, you learn how to stretch each recipe to its limits. Therefore, my mother's family developed other ways to present this recipe.

Here are two delicious ways to serve the polenta. One of my mother's favorite ways to serve it like lasagna. Take a large platter. Cut the leftover polenta into triangles and compose layers of polenta, cheese, and sauce. When finished, put in the oven. Let it cook for about twenty minutes or until the cheese is thoroughly melted over the polenta. Another way to make polenta is to fry it. Take a frying pan and cover it with olive oil. Cut the polenta into triangular pieces. Take any cheese you have in the house. As I mentioned before, Munster cheese blends particularly well with the polenta. It seems to bring the earthiness of the cornmeal out. Fry the polenta with the cheese is completely melted. As a child, when I that fried polenta was my lunch, I would not walk but run home.

Polenta is one of the ultimate comfort foods for a cold winter's day.

The use of potatoes is was my mother's invention. It softens the texture of the polenta.

Ravioli's with Mushroom Filling

One of the great treasures of Northern Italian cuisine is Ravioli. Who knew a little square of pasta filled with various surprises could bring such culinary delight and glee and make us clamor like children for a taste? As the years progressed, the northern Italians became magnificently proficient in presenting the world with more delectable and unforgettable fillings. That being said, for many years, the mundane cheese version has been the only one known to the masses. It is only in the not too distant past, that new variations for the stuffing have been shared with the world.

This mushroom version which I will present to you shortly, is actually one of my mother's inventions. She devised this recipe from one of the rare meals she had outside of the confines of her home. My mother's home, where she has settled since 1961, sits on Mahan Avenue which is comfortably in the Pelham Bay Section of the Bronx. The is the name for Pelham Bay Park. Pelham Bay Park in New York has the great distinction of being New York's largest park. It resides on the neighborhood's northeastern border. The majority of this land was purchased by Thomas Pell in 1654. It was part of an original grant to Dutch West India Company Italian, Irish, Greek, and German populations have called Pelham Bay their home for numerous years. In recent years, there has been a massive influx of Hispanics and to a lesser extent African- Americans and Asians. On Saturday, she was at one of the many Italian dances she frequented during the year. My mother with her usual sigh, though, "not another dish of cheese ravioli." Famished, she grudgingly placed the ravioli on her fork and bit gingerly into it. To her surprise, a glorious and innovative ingredient knocked on her taste buds. She knew it as the constant companion that resided by her side in the kitchen. It was the porcini mushroom. At last, her fellow brethren in the kitchen have finally discovered the powerful flavor of the porcini mushroom and the complementary effect it would have on pasta, particularly when it is used in pasta as a filling.

My mother, never one to deter from a cooking challenge, decided that she would reproduce this recipe at home. Though my mother was plagued with various insecurities, they did not extend to the kitchen. Therefore, she would have no reservations or fear in reconstructing this recipe. As you will see from the recipe, my mother decided that combining the porcini mushrooms with its various family members such as Button and Portobello and inviting them to the party would prove to do the trick. Since their flavor tends to be strong, please do not use too many types of mushrooms for this recipe. Three is a good number.

RECIPE

INGREDIENTS

Porcini Mushrooms (½ a cup)

Button Mushrooms (1 Box)

Portobello Mushrooms (1 Box)

Eggs (4 Eggs)

Bread Crumbs (2 Handfuls)

Parmesan Cheese (2 Handfuls)

Garlic (3 Cloves)

Bouillon Cube (½ A Cube)

Butter (A Quarter of A Stick)

Oil (Enough to Cover the Bottom of The Pan)

Nutmeg (1 Teaspoon)

UTENSILS

Bowl (1)

Big Frying Pan (1)

Big Spoon (1)

First peel and cut your garlic into pieces. After you have finished cutting your garlic, put it aside. You will need it later on. Remove your button and Portobello Mushrooms from their Boxes. You would wash your Portobello and Button mushrooms and grate them. Then take your porcini mushrooms and put them in water to soften them. When they have completed softening, you would then chop them. Take your frying pan with your heat on high, add your quarter stick of butter, enough oil to cover your pan garlic, ½ bouillon cube, and nutmeg. Place them into the frying pan. When the butter has been melted, take your grated Button and Portobello mushrooms and add them to the pan. Let them sauté on high heat for five minutes. After the five minutes, add your porcini mushrooms and continue to keep your heat on high for an additional five minutes. Let your mushrooms then cook for about a half an hour. This will also enable all the water to be released from the mushrooms. Five minutes before you had completed cooking the mushrooms, add two handfuls of bread crumbs. Continue cooking until your bread crumbs are totally dissolved. This will help to bind all the ingredients together. After your bread crumbs have dissolved, remove your mushrooms from your pan and put them in a bowl to cool. When they have sufficiently cooled, you would add your two handfuls of parmesan cheese, your yolk of two eggs and two whole eggs. The eggs are vital in binding your ingredients. Mix all these ingredients thoroughly with your hands. Always remember your hands are your best tools. There is your filling!

Be forewarned. Unlike the various other Ravioli recipes I will introduce you to in this book, when making this recipe you will only need a small portion to fill each ravioli. This, because of the strong flavor of the mushroom combination that makes up this filling.

Ravioli with Butternut Squash Filling

As I am writing this recipe, I am brought back to a simpler time. A time when in my little world, an easy bake oven was the only thing that remotely connected me with my mother in the cooking department. When I was born, the cooking umbilical cord seemed to have been severed too severely. It would take several years before it would be repaired. As a young child, I would sit on my bed and fantasize that I would one day be the recipient of my mother's cooking ability.

My mother's cooking could be reviewed as a Rolex watch. It was a generational heirloom and I wanted to help it keep giving and giving. I would often fantasize about putting my blueprint on the many recipes in my mother's possession. It was also during these moments that I came to realize that her recipes needed no enhancement. During these times, I experienced my first feelings of awe of the magical powers my mother processed in the kitchen. I tried to convince myself the reason I was not yet comparable to my mother in the kitchen was that she had her utensils disguised as a magic wand and the various herbs she used were potions. Later in life, when I was no longer engrossed in my childhood fantasies. I realized, that my mother was an artist. Unlike a professional artist who uses a paintbrush, my mother uses a spoon to create her masterpieces.

The first time my niece had the opportunity to try my mother's butternut squash ravioli, not being a great lover of butternut squash, or for that matter, any vegetable was not green, she was a bit apprehensive. My niece was a serious groupie of my mother's spinach ravioli. Like a lawyer, she would vehemently argue, to anyone that would listen, that there was no better fair than a dish of Nonna's spinach ravioli.

As my mother placed the dish before her, her face took on a distorted and quizzical form. She slowly picked up the fork and gingerly bit into the ravioli. As she demurely and politely chewed. A smile slowly appeared across her face and made a reassuring sound of approval. She then proceeded to finish her meal. Through the years, in my niece's eyes, though the spinach ravioli remains in first place, the butternut squash is a formidable runner -up.

RECIPE

INGREDIENTS

Butternut Squash (I Medium Sized One)

Spinach (1 Cup)

Butter (2 Pats of Butter)

Ricotta (1 Carton)

Mascarpone (1 Carton)

Oil (3 Tablespoons)

Bouillon Cube (1)

Nutmeg (1 Teaspoon)

Garlic (3 Cloves)

Parsley (2 Teaspoons)

Parmesan cheese (3 Handfuls)

Bread crumbs (2 Handfuls)

Eggs (2 Whole Eggs)

UTENSILS

Frying Pan (One)

Big Bowl (One)

Big Spoon (One)

Peel your garlic and cut into pieces. Take your butternut squash and cut into pieces. Take your frying pan. Add enough olive oil to cover the frying pan, your pat of butter and one bouillon cube to the pan. Heat your pan on high for about three minutes. Add your pieces of butternut squash and garlic. Let the squash cook until it develops a pudding-like consistency. When you see you have obtained this consistency, put your squash to the side. You would then take your spinach and boil it. When it is cooked, you would strain it and then chop it. You would then take your frying pan and once again add enough oil to cover your pan, your other pat of butter and your teaspoon of nutmeg. Add both your spinach and butternut squash and stir them thoroughly in your pan. Five minutes before you are done, add your bread crumbs. As you know, this will bind your ingredients. After you have completed cooking this, put it in a bowl on the side to let it cool. When it has cooled, you would take a big bowl. Add your squash, spinach, carton of mascarpone and carton of ricotta and your two eggs. You need to mix these ingredients thoroughly. As with the bread crumbs, the eggs will bind your ingredients. After you completed mixing these ingredients thoroughly, you would then add your two cups of parmesan cheese and mix it in thoroughly. Lastly, you would add your parmesan cheese and mix it in thoroughly. There is you filling.

Ravioli's with Spinach and Ricotta

This ravioli is the most requested food item on my mother's imaginary kitchen blackboard. Meaning, it is automatically presented and never needs to be directly requested.

The making of these ravioli's began in my family when my mother was thirteen years old. Because of the hard times and poverty created by the war, a pasta machine was a distant dream. So, they were forced to call upon their physical stamina and the prehistoric cooking instrument known as the rolling pin. Though a daunting task, the mouth-watering result and all the compliments that awaited them were all the desired ammunition they needed to prompt them to forge on and continue to make these square treasures.

As with all the recipes I am writing in this book, I automatically transported back in time to my mother's kitchen. As a young girl, I would be the final link in the assembly line that would produce these wonderful edible pillows. My mother, my godmother and I would designate various Saturdays during the course of the year to make ravioli. We would rise at dawn and begin our adventure which would take up most of the day. It is during these times, I would often recall my mother and godmother reminiscing of how poor they were and how they would often turn the most meager culinary supplies into marvelous creations. It was also during these times that a strong bond would form between all of us. A bond created not only stories of despair but also of hilarious mishaps which we have encountered in our lives.

My godmother was designated with the job of making the pasta. A job she was quite well practiced in. She used a pasta machine attached to a baby high chair from the 1950's. After all these years, it remains the main and most proficient tool in making the ravioli. My godmother made the pasta and gingerly cut it into pieces. She took the pasta and passed it through the machine. She repeated this procedure three times for every piece of pasta. This resulted in long strips of glorious pasta. My mother's job was to take spoonful of the filling and place it on the sheet of pasta. She would place the filling about an inch apart and then fold the pasta over. Then, it was my turn. I made a crease between each spoonful of filling, cut them into a ravioli shape and place them in a pan. When the pan is cover with these little treasures, I would place a piece of saran wrap between each layer then totally cover it with the aluminum foil. We would make about four pans and then freeze them. We put them in bags after they were thoroughly frozen. This was done more so due to space constraints than anything else. We would do this at least five times a year.

These wonderful and edible pillows continue to grace the table at family gatherings not only on holidays but other days during the year. The other days of the year, this ravioli is primarily served at the request of my mother's grandchildren. Like all grandmothers, they would never deny their grandchildren anything. To this day, this dish transports me back to when I was with my mother and godmother in the kitchen constructing this wonderful ravioli. Also, as an adult, I find these memories to be a potent help in enabling me to endure the most trying times of my life. Grazie, Mama.

⁓ *Lynn Tiramani* ⁓

RECIPE

INGREDIENTS

Frying Pan (One)

Box of Spinach (1)

Ricotta (1 pound which is equivalent to one carton of ricotta)

Oil (3 Tablespoons)

Butter (2 Pats)

Chicken Bouillon (1 Cube)

Nutmeg (1 Teaspoon)

Garlic (3 Cloves)

Parmesan Cheese (3 to 4 Handfuls)

Bread Crumbs (2 Handfuls)

Eggs (2 Whole Eggs)

UTENSILS

Large Bowl (One)

You would begin by boiling your spinach. When it has completed cooking, you would strain it and chop it. Take your oil, as always, make sure you use enough to cover the bottom of the frying pan. You would then add your garlic, butter and nutmeg in a frying pan. You have the heat under your pan on high heat for about five minutes. When you pan is sufficiently heated. You would then add your spinach to your frying pan and sauté for about two minutes then add the two handfuls of bread crumbs. You need to stir your bread crumbs until they had dissolved in the spinach. This would take approximately twenty minutes. You add the bread crumbs because they are a vital ingredient in helping to bind all the ingredients together. After you have finished sautéing your spinach, set it aside in a bowl to let it cool. After it has completely cooled, place it in a big bowl and add ricotta, parmesan cheese, cream cheese and two whole eggs mix it all together thoroughly. The Eggs are mixed in to bind the ingredients. There is your filling.

Tortolini in Brodo (Soup)

Of all my mother recipes, this one heightened my admiration for my mother's culinary skills even more. I learned very early while watching my mother prepare these round, tasty treats, that you must be instilled with a true love for cooking to enjoy laboring in the kitchen for hours on end. To say that this recipe is time intensive is an understatement. If you do not have at least two days of your life to dedicate to this endeavor, I advise you to not even pursue it.

As with the ravioli, this is also an assembly line venture. The three major characters remain the same. Once again, my mother, my godmother and I are called upon to bring this recipe to life. Our labors, would ultimately lead to a finale which almost always garners rave reviews.

Due to the labor intensiveness of this recipe, these round delights were primarily served during the holidays. When these tortellini are offered to guests, their eyes usually filled with all the wide- eyed wonder, delight and vigor of a child on Christmas morning. Trust me, before your guests finish their last bite, they will already be thinking about asking for the dish to be on next year's Christmas menu.

While I am writing this recipe, the corners of my mouth slowly form into a smile. My thoughts are quickly transported to memories of past family gatherings that revolved around the ingestion of these tasty wonders. Having six grandchildren in the family, much of the chatter centered on their everyday activities and various little troubles that plagued them. Troubles which were often met with sensitive understanding which helped to remove the band- aide hiding all the teenage insecurity and would eventually enable them to continue on their long journey to adulthood. It was also during these times that family matters which involved the adults were brought to the forefront. We often found that discussing family matters at the dinner table enabled the participants to deal with these issues in a manner that was often met with laughter, some serious banter, and ultimately resolution. Being of Italian descent, it is our birthright and our feeling that there is no better place to discuss the ills of life then at the dinner table. This would often lead me to think that the leaders of the world should follow that path. I feel many of the world's ills would be resolved over a great plate of food.

My cousin's daughter would often tell me she would wish that every Sunday was a major holiday so that she could have Tortellini in Brodo. Prior to going to visit her Nonna, she would place a call a week ahead of time requesting these round delights. Nonna being Nonna would always accommodate her request.

RECIPE

INGREDIENTS

Veal (1 Pound)
Quarts of Stock (2)
Pork (1 pound)
Bread Crumbs (2 Handfuls)
Stalk of Celery (1)
Parmesan (2 Cups)
Eggs (4 Eggs – 2 Whole and 2 Yolks)
Nutmeg ½ Grated One
Garlic Cloves (3)
Onion (1)
Stalk of Celery (1)
Oil (Enough to cover Pan)

UTENSILS

Pot (One Medium Size)
Frying Pan (One)
Bowl (One)

Bouillon (1 Cube)

As I indicated, this recipe takes about two days to make. On your first day, you would begin by taking your frying pan and coat the bottom with oil. You would add your veal and pork to the frying pan with your onions, garlic cloves and nutmeg and two quarts of stock and celery. You would cook this for four hours. Also, while this is cooking, make sure you have a pot of water boiling on the side boiling, because while your veal and pork are cooking, you may see your water reducing, that is what you will be using the boiled water for. After your veal and pork have completed cooking, you would remove it from your pot and then chop it or if you wish, you may pass it through your food processor. By the time you have completed this, your meat should have almost a pudding consistency. You would then take your meat and put it in your frying pan. It is at this point that you would add your bread crumbs and let it cook in the pan for about 10 minutes. Then you would take it out of your frying pan and transfer it to your bowl and let it cool. You would cover it and put in your refrigerator overnight. The next day, you would take it out and add your eggs and parmesan cheese. Remember the eggs are used to bind your ingredients. You would mix it thoroughly and there is your filling.

Risotto

I initially introduced you to this recipe at the beginning of this book because it the first recipe served at my family's home. Primarily, because the simple ingredients used in this recipe such as the onions, garlic, and leek were gifts that their homeland's soil afforded them in great quantities. Especially, the prominent and vital ingredient in this recipe, which is the porcini mushroom. This product is primarily grown in Northern Italy. An abundance of this product could be found everywhere. Trust me there was never a fear of running out of it. Therefore, because of this reason and its deliciousness, it proved to be the perfect signature dish of the restaurant. It is also one of the gold standard recipes of Northern Italian cooking. It is, in my mind, one of the first and most popular recipes transported from Northern Italy to the land of the free.

Now as I fast- forwarded in time and I am in the process of writing this recipe, I can hear my mother's accent tinged voice informing me that my niece Christine was coming over and that we had to make risotto. This was my cue to gather the ingredients for this Italian comfort food. Like my nephew with Polenta, Risotto was it for Christine. Risotto was my Niece's caviar. If there were leftovers, my niece would eagerly take them and enjoy than another day.

While our southern Italian counterparts would have pasta on Sundays, we would have risotto. Risotto was the first recipe I learned to cook. When it is cooked correctly, the casual cook might find it a little tedious and labor- intensive. Particularly having to stand over your rice and repeatedly adding the soup. But I assure you, it is well worth the time and effort. As any cook knows, when starting a new recipe, the first attempts never quite live up to the original. Eventually, through practice, you will be able to duplicate this recipe.

As with all my mother's recipes, this was handed down the various generations of her family. My mother being the creative cook and always looking to enhance recipes, would, through the years, add her own twist to this recipe. One particular twist which I thoroughly enjoyed was cubes of pancetta. Pancetta is Italy's version of bacon. Should you decide to use this ingredient, it should be added at the same time as the porcini mushrooms.

RECIPE

INGREDIENTS

Chicken Bouillon Cube (1)

Onions (3)

Oil (Enough to cover base)

Stock of Leek (1)

Pieces of Garlic (5)

Pat of Butter (1)

Porcini mushrooms (1 Handful)

Chicken Soup (1 Pot Full Medium Size)

Chicken Leg (1)

UTENSILS

Big Pot (One)

Small Pot (One)

Ladle (One)

You would first chop your onions, leek and garlic. Your porcini mushrooms have a rough exterior and need to be softened. You put do that by soaking them in a glass of water. You would take your pot and cover the base of the pot with your oil. You would then add your chicken bouillon cube and pat of butter. Set the heat on high and let it heat for five minutes. After the five minutes, add your onions, garlic and leek. Stir all these ingredients together. Midway through the cooking process, raise your heat add the porcini mushrooms. Stir for about five minutes continuing to have your heat on high. After letting that sauté for five minutes, add your water from the porcini and let it boil on rapidly for five minutes. If you have it, add a chicken leg at this point. This is optional. Cover the pot and lower the heat. Remember to stir occasionally. You don't want the ingredients to burn. Let all these ingredients cook for about an hour. The onions need to cook very thoroughly. You would then add your rice and your chicken soup. Continue to add the chicken soup each time the rice finishes absorbing it. Continue this process until the rice is cooked. The rice should take about twenty minutes to cook.

The Evolution of Pasta and machinery used to make pasta

My mother was introduced to pasta making at the age of 14. Unlike my godmother, due to the loss of her mother, she started cooking at the age of 10. This procedure would often be performed at a big round table stationed directly in the middle of the kitchen, which in many Italian homes, was considered the center of the universe.

The mechanism that was used to compose the various forms of pasta, was rustic, to say the least. As per my mother's description, I viewed this piece as having all the characteristics of the old house that had established permanent residency in my backyard. A piece of apparatus that had three different blades that would enable you to compose the type of pasta you wanted for that day. It was stationed directly on a 1957 high chair. Though this pasta mechanism was extremely provincial, it would ably get the job done. Upon reflection, my admiration grew for my mother and my ancestors. Through the years I had come to realized that they were able to accomplish the most arduous tasks regarding cooking with such provincial mechanisms.

You would fill this apparatus, which had a handle with pasta and turn the handle back and forth to crank out the pasta. This was used for many years until an upgraded and modern version made life simpler for the masses. The upgraded version possessed three slots which dictated the various sizes of the pasta. This upgraded version also enabled them to produce mass quantities at a time. The additional quantities would be put in the freezer to embrace future ravioli fillings.

Pasta

The pasta making process began in my family with my great-grandmother. Like any prized family jewel, this heirloom was handed down to my grandmother and her sisters and eventually took a detour to my mother's kitchen. Due to the times, and scarcity of money, they were delegated to using primitive tools to create the pasta. A rolling - pin which had all the resemblance of a disfigured walking cane, was their main culinary tool. As the reader can surmise from my last statement, the absence of a pasta machine lengthened the process considerably. I am often inclined to believe that the sweat used in making this wonderful blanket for ravioli fillings, contributed to the life span of my ancestors.

When I think of pasta, it brings me back to a simpler time in my childhood. I am immediately transported back to the kitchen in the basement of our three- family house. Before my eyes, a picture flashes of two women in house dresses and scarves securely tied around their forehead. The air is filled with the sounds of a language which no longer exists, conveyed in a rapid- fire fashion. It is during this time that the hidden stories of the past are finally brought to life. Stories, that comprised of the many struggles endured during a war which filled the atmosphere of the majority of their growing years. Surprisingly, through all the madness, there were even stories that propelled a very uncommon and forgotten response, laughter. My mother would often stress how they would embrace the cherish and rare commodity of laughter. Laughter enabled them to endure these trying times.

For me, I viewed these times as a bonding session not only with my godmother and mother, but also the heritage that made up part of my being. It was through these times that I truly became acquainted not only of their existence but also how they conquered the perils of their life during war- torn Italy. I found myself marveling at the resiliency of a people. Though engulfed in the depths of conflict, they were still able to maintain a sense of visibility through such turbulent times. Not only did the war make them magnificently versed in creating culinary wonders due to being forced to use meager supplies, but it also instilled them with an unparallel survival instinct. A survival instinct that would ultimately enable them to pursue their dreams of obtaining a better life in America.

RECIPE

INGREDIENTS
Flour– 3 Pounds

Eggs (6 Whole Eggs)

Hot Water (1 Cup)

Salt (3 Teaspoons)

UTENSILS
A big Board

A large Kitchen Table

Place the cutting board on a table and pour the flour directly on it. In the middle of the flour, pour water and put three eggs in the water. It should resemble a pool in the middle of the flour. Add the salt. Mix everything together gently. Mix until you obtain almost a silly putty consistency. When the mixture is this consistency, place it in a bowl and cover it with any kitchen clear paper for an hour. That is how you make pasta dough.

The Evolution of Pasta and machinery used to make pasta

My mother was introduced to pasta making at the age of 14. Unlike my godmother, due to the loss of her mother, she commenced at the age of 10. This procedure would often be performed at a big round table stationed directly in the middle of the kitchen. Which in many Italian homes was considered the center of the universe. And when completed was, laid to dry on the various beds.

The mechanism that was used to compose the various forms of pasta, such as angel hair pasta and the coats used to house the pasta, was rustic, to say the least. As per my mother's description, I personally viewed this piece as having all the characteristics of the old house that had established permanent residency in my backyard. Though this pasta hose was extremely provincial, it would ably get the job done. Upon reflection, my admiration grew for my mother and my ancestors. Through the years I had come to realized that they were able to accomplish the most arduous tasks regarding cooking with such provincial mechanisms.

You would fill this hose with the pasta. The hose had a handle. You would turn the handle back and forth and crank out the pasta. This was used for many years until an upgraded and modern version made life simpler for the masses. The upgraded version possessed three slots which dictated the various sizes of the pasta. This upgraded version also enabled them to produce mass quantities at a time. The additional quantities would be put in the freeze to embrace future ravioli fillings.

Torta

Another one of the ultimate comfort foods of Northern Italy is Torta. It is given this title not only because of its great capacity to warm the soul but it also has the ability of making one forget about the rigors of the day. The main ingredient potatoes proved to be a substantial cure to squash the frequent hunger bangs that stirred the workers during the course of their day. This was also easy to transport. This was vital to the common everyday worker. Torta also proved to be an economic lifesaver because of its heartiness and proved to have a great deal of staying power to be enjoyed for many glorious meals ahead.

As I am writing this recipe, a giggle emanates from my being. I remember how my mother's many friends would try to outdo each other with their various versions of their own Torta recipes. For some unearthly reason, Torta always brought out the best in the competitive cooking spirit among them. Needless to say, first prize would be won by all. The end products were always so delicious that everyone was a winner.

The birthplace of Torta is Parma, which is a close neighbor to the town of Piacenza where, as you know, my mother spent her formidable years. The cooks of Piacenza were known to make there Torta with one ingredient which was potatoes. The cooks of Parma where much more adventurous. They would make their Torta with various ingredients, such as rice, spinach and squash. The experiment of using various ingredients enabled them to incorporate healthy foods for their children who would often play hide and seek when they knew a green substance would be waiting for them in their dish.

Lynn Tiramani

RECIPE

INGREDIENTS

Potatoes (4 Pounds)

Garlic (3 Gloves)

Onions (3 Onions)

Leeks (2 Stalks)

Oil (4 Tablespoons)

Butter (½ Stick)

Chicken Bouillon Cube (1)

Pepper (1 Teaspoon)

Nutmeg (A Pinch)

Handfuls Of Bread Crumbs (3)

Pinch Of Sugar (1)

Egg (1)

UTENSILS

Frying Pan (One Large)

Big Serving Platter (One)

Big Inch Deep Pan (One)

Your first step is that you must make a sauce. Have a small pot of soup boiling on the side because you are going to add it to your ingredients. Put your oil, butter and a bouillon cube in a frying pan, heat on high until dissolved. (Ask about when to put the soup in), Add the garlic, onions, leeks, nutmeg and pepper and stir them together. Let all the ingredients cook to a mushy consistency. Cook the potatoes on the side. When your potatoes are cooked, strain and mash them. Put the bread crumbs on the bottom of the pan and sprinkle oil on them. Spread the mash potatoes which you have combined with the on top of the bread crumbs. Beat an egg with a pinch of sugar. Spread it on top of the mashed potatoes. Make sure you spread it evenly. This combination in the pan is your actual torta. Put the pan with your Torta in the oven and heat at 350 degrees. It will take between a half to 45 minutes or until it is golden brown.

Fritatta

I call this meal, the portable manna from heaven for Italian school children. It was what occupied our Partridge family lunch box. It was our peanut butter and jelly. Italian mothers often viewed peanut butter and jelly as not having the regal stature of frittata. Therefore, it would never grace the middle of the two pieces of bread that filled the sandwiches of their children. It would not be until my high school years, through much deliberation and debate, I was able to eventually convince my mother of the great attributes and benefits of the American powerhouse protein which we call peanut butter. To this day, I continue to be privileged to have both my Italian and American culinary alter egos satisfied through these two wonderful foods.

As I am writing this, visions of a stark and bland cafeteria stationed in the Northeast section of the Bronx flash before me. My eyes quickly revert to the back corner of the room to a fair- haired girl. I remember how this fair- haired girl would make a point to position herself firmly in the fold of the in- crowd. A crowd, which I was never given a formal invitation to be a part of. Primarily because I did not possess all that attributes such as beauty, brains and monetary statue that would ever warrant my membership in such a crowd. So, with that being said, I often wondered why she would securely plant herself next to me at lunchtime. Eventually, I came to realize that is was not me but the Frittata that propelled her to even venture close to my space. After many countless days of eyeing my afternoon nourishment, I eventually decided to part with half my sandwich and offered it to her. Her immense joy while eating the frittata was all too apparent in the way she hurriedly devoured the sandwich. She gave the sandwich rave reviews and shared this discovery with the rest of her posse. As the days passed, she and her posse would take turns in planting themselves directly in the space next to me expecting a piece of my manna from heaven. Not only do I extend my gratitude to Frittata for turning the school misfit into Ms. Popularity but for also for a friendship the remains relevant to this day.

The history of Frittata stems all the way back to my great, great-grandmother. She helped to give birth to how the recipe evolved through the branches of my family tree and how it eventually cooked by the family today. The very simple combination of eggs, parsley, and parmesan cheese proved to be the perfect recipe. This manner of making Frittata continued up until later in my mother's life. But all that changed, when one day, she found herself in an unforeseen circumstance. My brother and his family unexpectedly came for a visit. My mother wanted to make frittata. Unfortunately, she did not have parmesan cheese. Like every good cook, she just used the remaining ingredients and hoped for the best. When she finished cooking her simpler and revised recipe, she served it and was met with hearty adulation. The response convinced her to continue to prepare it in the same manner going forward.

Now, I will give you the opportunity to prepare it in your own home. Enjoy making it. Let your children get involved. Have them be your sue chef.

La Cucina della mia Bisnonna

RECIPE

INGREDIENTS

Eggs (5 Whole Eggs)

Onions (4)

Salt (1 Teaspoon)

Parsley (2 Tablespoons)

Parmesan (1 Handful, Optional)

Oil (Enough to cover pan)

UTENSILS

Frying Pan (One

Large Bowl (One)

Spatula (One)

Fork (One)

Finely chop the onions. Crack the eggs into a bowl. Mix in the parsley and parmesan cheese. If you prefer, you may do what my mother did, and not add the parmesan cheese. I promise it will be just as good. Thoroughly mix the ingredients. After it is thoroughly mixed, put the mixture aside. Add oil to the frying pan. Turn your heat on high add the chopped onions. Keep the heat on high for about five minutes. Then lower the heat and cover the onions until thoroughly cooked. This will take about 45 minutes. Periodically, take the cover off and stir the onions. When the onions are cooked, slowly add the egg, parsley and parmesan (optional) mixture into the pan. Let it cook in the pan for about 3 minutes. Cut the egg mixture into four pieces with a spatula. Turn the pieces over and let it cook on that side for about three minutes. Continue to turn over until cooked to your taste.

Grandfather Giovanni's Lamb Recipe

My great- grandfather, Giovanni was the architect of this recipe. He was my grandmother, Linda's father. He was welcomed into this world in 1868 in the town of Picenza, Italy. He was third of three boys in the line of siblings which included three brothers and two sisters. My great grandparents were married in 1890. Their first child was born in 1892 and would have seven more. Besides assisting my grandmother with the culinary duties in the little restaurant which they opened at the beginning of the 20th century, my grandfather's main profession was making salami. A profession which had been handed down from generation to generation. A skill which he had been paid handsomely for by the locals. His family recipe was so pleasing to the palate that it warranted his participation in the many salami competitions which were held both in Milan and Paris. The judges of these events concurred with the masses and he always departed with the gold medal. Being the humble man that he was, he often discarded this talent as not particularly astounding and that anyone was capable of creating a salami. My grandfather continued pleasing the masses until he was called to heaven in 1944.

Since this recipe, like every precious heirloom was handed down through the generations, his sons and grandson can continue the practice of introducing this culinary delight to forthcoming generations. Being part of the forthcoming generations, my brother and I had the great pleasure of having our taste buds be the recipient of this wonderful culinary delight. On the few excursions in which my brother and I ventured to Italy with my mother, one of the most anticipated reasons in which we were delighted to travel to the land of our ancestors, was not to see family, but to reacquaint ourselves with the salami. Me being a six- year old and my brother was ten at that time, while in Italy, would stay at my grandfather's house. A new house which was funded by the earnings my father obtained in his Adoptive land of America. This modern structure, in a primarily medieval land, was surrounded by a massive piece of green. I remember this massive green primarily beneficial in providing both me and my brother with a massive playground. But, the most important item which was housed in this modern structure, was the room which contained the salami. A memory which remains with me regarding this bread accompaniment, is that my brother always seemed to know exactly which room the salami was hanging him. This top -secret information, given him the opportunity to partake in even greater quantity than the rest of us. By getting to it first, he would eat a quantity of it, prior to exposing it to the rest of us. Years later, my uncle confessed to me, that he was my brother informant regarding the whereabouts of the humble room which housed the infamous salami. It figures! But I digress, back to the recipe at hand. Just wanted to give you, my dear reader, a glimpse into a memory regarding one of many delicious food sonata's beside the lamb composed with my grandfather's wonderful hands.

In Italy, holidays are considered the most culinary important time of the year for a home chef to show their cooking prowess. One of those holidays, being Easter. One year, as Easter approached, lamb being the preferred fare that is served on this occasion, my grandfather decided to alter his usual recipe into something different. Although the way he had been cooking the lamb was always well received by the masses, it was time for a change. On the Saturday before Easter, he ventured into the backyard behind the restaurant where all the primary ingredients for the recipes were grown. Though not usually baffled as to what ingredients to use, he was with lamb. He was hoping a few of the various herbs that grow there would magically call out to him and indicate they were the perfect enhancement to lamb. After an hour of standing and much deliberation, he decided on the old reliables of garlic and rosemary. As all good cooks, his intuition was correct. He hit the jackpot. The masses that crammed his small restaurant that Easter, loved it. Eventually, it became such a big hit, that it was requested not only on Easter but other times of the year.

RECIPE

INGREDIENTS

Lamb Cut to Pieces (1 Pound)
Cloves of Garlic Chopped (3)
Chopped Rosemary (1 Tablespoon)
Butter (A Pat)
Chicken Bouillon Cube (One)
Oil (Enough to Cover Bottom Of Pan)
Parsley (5 Tablespoons)
Chicken Soup (1 ½ Cup)

UTENSILS

Small Pot (One)
Medium Pot (One)

You would first chop your garlic and rosemary together. Take your pan and add your oil and butter. Take your pan and add enough oil to cover bottom of pan. Put your heat on high and to your pan add your rosemary, garlic, and lamb. First, let your lamb sauté on high heat in your pan for ten minutes. Then cover your pan and lower your heat. Let your lamb simmer for about an hour. While your lamb is simmering, have a pan of chicken stock boiling on the side. This boiling chicken stock will be added to lamb because during the cooking process the lamb tends to get dry. Continue to add the chicken soup as each time the lamb has completed absorbing it but please make sure at the end of the recipe the soup is not totally absorbed. You don't want it soupy but you want to have a little sauce left. Sprinkle your parsley ten minutes before the lamb has completed cooking.

Great Grandmother Maria's Veal

My great- grandmother was the true architect of many of the recipes which flood the pages of this book. You see, her cooking aptitude and passion was transported and continues to live through my mother. To this day, her spirit continues to live through the plat of this recipe.

This veal dish which I am about to introduce you to, bears the basic ingredient foundation for the majority of the recipes in this book. This foundation was the brainchild of my great- grandmother, Maria. Many of these ingredients were grown in the small patch of land which said securely sat behind her humble abode. Like every good cook, my great- grandmother had an astute knack of combining the simplest ingredients to any dish and turning into fare fit for a king. While I was growing up, this recipe, because of its importance in the household menu line, was primarily served on Sunday. As children, we felt like Halloween was every Sunday because we always had a special treat.

During my childhood, I would often be the shadow hovering behind my mother in our small, rectangular kitchen. I would be tucking at her apron begging her to employ me as her Sous chef. I promised her I would not hand her over to the authorities for illegally putting a minor to work. I reiterated the fact that I was of Italian descent and what is in the family stays in the family. My mother, after having her fill of my badgering, finally relented. She would first always remind of the tears that would be prompted by the onions I chopped. Hoping, primarily that this would dissuade me from wanting to participate in the preparation. I assured her, I was on a mission and nothing was going to deter me from my destiny. After much practice, I would obtain a great proficiency in the art of chopping. My mother finally, becoming confident in my skills, christened me with the title Sous Chef.

It was during these times that my mother would divulge information about her childhood. I treasured these moments because I was given a glimpse into how the human spirit continued to march on in times of unspeakable despair. About being a young girl during the war and how they would seek shelter from their unwelcomed guests, the German soldiers whose main purpose was to soil their yet untouched person. My mother was one of the fortunate ones, she was always able to escape. It was at this interval during the story that she would put her head down and say there were others not as lucky. She would reiterate about how these scared young women would never recover from the emotional scars which were residue from this unrequested interlude. My mother also said how she was extremely grateful that the people of her town possessed a heart of compassion and understanding as opposed to banishment towards these young women. A rear commodity in a time of moral steadfastness. I also remember my mother cringing as she spoke of the bombs that infiltrated her town. How she often had the fear of the legs which transported her to shelter would buckle under and she would never reach her destination. But she always did. She felt that the Grandmother she never knew was running beside her and guiding her to safety. To this day, because of this experience, she will never pose at a channel which is transmitting a War story. Her reasoning, "Linda, I lived it, I don't need to see it."

This veal recipe which I am about to introduce you to was one of the first recipes I learned primarily because it was one of my palate's favorites. This was the second recipe which I mastered. Though it took many tries, I finally master it. Though, not very complimentary, it was good enough for my mother to declare that it was better than hers.

RECIPE

INGREDIENTS

Veal (1 Pound cut in cubes)

Onions (3 Onions)

Celery (2 Sticks)

Garlic (4 Cloves)

Parsley (To Taste)

Leek (½ of Stalk)

Bouillon Cube (1 Small)

Tomato Paste (2 Tablespoon)

Homemade Soup (2 Cups Boiling in Pot)

Oil (Enough to Cover Bottom Of Pan)

UTENSILS

Big (Pot)

Spoon (One Big to Stir)

You would marinate your chopped veal with rosemary, salt and pepper and have it marinate overnight in your refrigerator.

Chop your onions, celery, garlic, parsley and leek. You would take your pan and add enough oil to cover bottom of pan and add your small chicken bouillon cube. On high heat add your onions, celery, garlic, parsley and leek. Stir all these ingredients on high for about five minutes. After the five minutes, lower your heat putting your cover on letting your ingredients cook between 45 minutes to an hour. After all your ingredients are cooked, increase your heat again to high and add your veal. Keep that heat on high for 10 minutes then lower your heat and let your veal cook for a half an hour. Then once again, increase your heat on high and add about ½ cup of soup and the two tablespoons of tomato sauce. Keep your heat on high until the tomato paste dissolves. Lower your heat. Put your cover on your pot but do not completely cover it. Please leave a half an inch from the edge. Keep adding the rest of the remaining soup. Each time you see soup evaporating, add your soup again. You do this, because at the end you want a little sauce left, you don't want it to completely evaporate. Your veal will cook an additional hour and a half. Making total cooking time of two hours.

Louisa's Rainy Day Chicken Recipe

I call this the rainy-day chicken recipe, primarily, because it was developed on a rainy day. I remember as a young girl, it was a Friday afternoon. It was Easter recess so therefore; I was home from school. It was about 1:00 in the afternoon and my mother was contemplating what to make for dinner. She opened the refrigerator and her eyes immediately fell on the chicken. Her eyes then wandered over to her old reliable standby onions, leek, and celery. Her eyes then reverted to the cabinet before her. She opened it and the bottle of blackberry brandy stood boldly before her. She would cook all those ingredients and then add the chicken and at the end add the blackberry brandy. Wala!!! Louisa's chicken!

RECIPE

INGREDIENTS

Onions (3 Medium Size Chopped)

Garlic (3 Cloves Chopped)

Leek (2 Stalks)

Oil (Enough to Cover Pan)

Bouillon cube (½ Of a Large One)

Butter (1 Small Pat)

Salt (2 Teaspoons)

Pepper (A Pinch)

Rosemary (A Pinch)

UTENSILS

Frying Pans (Two Large)

Fork (One Big Fork)

Blackberry Brandy (1 Cup, Or Enough To Cover Your Chicken)

Leek (2 Stalks)

Chicken (1 Whole Chicken Cut In To Pieces)

You would begin by finely chopping your onions, garlic and leek. After you have finished chopping your ingredients, you would put them aside. Take your pot and put enough oil to cover the bottom of your pot, add your bouillon cube and pat of butter. Turn your heat on high, add your chopped onions, garlic and leek with salt, pepper and rosemary. Stir your ingredients for ten minutes keeping your heat on high. Cover your pan and let your onions cook thoroughly. This will take about an hour. When your onions are cooked add your chicken and let that cook for about an hour. Ten minutes before the chicken has completed cooking, add your blackberry brandy.

Nonna's Cod Fish Recipe

Although my mother had a treasure chest of great recipes, there were not many fish recipes. She personally does not like fish, so she was not very interested in pursuing ways in which to cook it. As you know, many Italians, on Christmas Eve serve some sort of fish. So, my mother keeping with that tradition, made sure she learned at least one recipe. The recipe which I am about to present to you comes from my Grandmother, Linda. My mother's mother. I personally love this.

RECIPE

INGREDIENTS

Onions (2)

Salt (A Dash)

Pepper (A Dash)

Tomato Paste (1 Teaspoon)

Oil (Enough to Cover Pan)

Flour (Enough to Cover the Pieces of Your Fish)

Cod Fish (2 Pounds)

Parsley (3 Tablespoons)

Paper Towels (A Roll)

UTENSILS

Big Frying Pan (1)

Fork (1)

Dish (1)

This recipe requires two days of preparation. As you know, Cod Fish is extremely salty, so you need to soak it in water. Your first day, you would soak your Cod Fish in water constantly draining it and adding new water. You do this because the Cod Fish is extremely salty and you want to make sure you rid it of as much salt as possible. The next day, just before you would begin the recipe, you would remove it from your water and dry your fish by patting it with a paper towel. You would then dip your fish in flour coating both sides. You would then take your frying pan. Coating the bottom of it with oil and brown both sides of your fish. After you have completed that, set your fish aside. You would then take your onions and garlic and chop them. After you have chopped them, you would take your frying pan and coat with oil adding your onions, garlic, salt and parsley. Just before your onions are completely cooked, which would take about 45 minutes to an hour, you would stir in your teaspoon of tomato paste. Then you would add your fish. Your fish would take between 30 and 45 minutes to cook.

Mom's Fish Filet Recipe

This is another one of my mother's three fish recipes. My mother wanted to develop a fish recipe which a person can do on a weeknight. A recipe which would not take a great deal of time or labor.

RECIPE

INGREDIENTS

Egg Wash (3 Eggs)
Salt (How Much)
Pepper (How Much)
Bread Crumbs (½ a Cup)
Garlic (3 Gloves)
Fish (5 Pieces)
Celery (1 Stalks)
Shallots (2 Small)
Leek (½ a Leek)

UTENSILS

Frying Pan (1 Large)
Dish (1 Large)
Fork (1)
Bowl (1 small)
Dish (1)
Frying Pan (1)
Knife (1)

Take your eggs, crack and beat into your small bowl for your egg wash. Take your fish and cover both sides of fish with egg wash and bread both sides of your fish. If you do homemade bread crumbs, you can add parsley and garlic to it. Cover this up with aluminum foil and put in the refrigerator. Take your Garlic, Celery, leeks, and shallots leeks or shallots and chop to obtain a fine texture. After you have finished doing that, take your frying pan and cover the bottom of the pan with your olive oil add your chopped ingredients and cook until tender. About 30 minutes. Then add your fish. Your fish should be cook in about 20 minutes.

Broccoli with an Italian Twist

RECIPE

INGREDIENTS

Broccoli (1 Box)

Olive Oil (Enough to cover pan)

Garlic (4 pieces chopped)

Parsley (2 Tablespoons)

Bouillon Cube (1 Cube)

Salt (1 Tablespoon)

UTENSILS

Medium Size Pot (1)

Medium Size Frying Pan (1)

Medium Size (Strainer)

Take your Broccoli out of the box. Take your medium- size pot. Add your water and tablespoon of salt. Bring your water to a boil. When your water has been brought to a boil, add your broccoli. Cook until tender. This should take about four to seven minutes or until tender. If you wish, you may also just take your frozen broccoli and place it in your water and cook right away. You do not have to boil the water first. When employing this method, it should take about 15 minutes. While your broccoli is cooking, chop your garlic and parsley. When your broccoli is cooked, strain it. Put your broccoli in a plate and put it aside. Take your frying pan and completely cover the bottom of it with your olive oil and add your bouillon cube, chopped garlic and parsley. Let your pan heat for about five minutes Then add your broccoli. Stir and sauté your broccoli until it is totally engulfed with the flavors of the garlic, parsley and oil.

Carrots

RECIPE

INGREDIENTS
Carrots (1 Pound)
Celery (2 Stalks)
Garlic (2 Cloves)
Salt (to taste)
Leek (2 Stalks)
Bouillon Cube (1)

UTENSILS
Medium Pot (1)
Frying Pan (1 Medium)
Spatula (1 Medium)

Wash your carrots. Skin them and cut in diagonal pieces. Fill your pot with water. Add your tablespoon of salt and two tablespoons of sugar. Add your carrots. You should cook them thoroughly. This should take approximately 20 minutes but the best way to check is to put a fork through them. If the fork slides easily through, they are cooked. While your carrots are cooking, chop your leek, garlic and celery. Take your frying pan. Coat the bottom with oil. Add your bouillon cube, leek, garlic and celery. These ingredients will take about twenty minutes to cook. When your carrots are cooked, drain them and put them aside. Add your cooked carrots to your leek, garlic and celery and sauté for five minutes and serve.

Peppers Alla Dina

RECIPE

INGREDIENTS

Orange Peppers (3)
Yellow Peppers (3)
Vinegar (1 Glass)
Oil (To Taste)
Salt (1 Tablespoon)
Sugar (2 Tablespoons)
Garlic (3 Cloves Cut Up)

UTENSILS

Medium Pot (1)
Fork (1)
Spoon (1)
Platter (1)

Take your peppers. Cut them diagonally. Add your water, glass of vinegar, tablespoon of salt, sugar and your peppers. Put your heat on high. When the water begins to boil, lower and add your peppers. During the cooking process, keep checking if you need additional salt or sugar. The peppers will take about twenty minutes or until they are al dente. When they are cooked, strain them. Pour them into your platter and season them with oil, garlic and salt to taste.

Ossobuco

RECIPE

INGREDIENTS

Onions (2 Small)

Celery (2 Stalks)

Garlic (3 Cloves)

Chicken Stock (2 Small Pots)

Rosemary (Enough to Cover Your Meat)

Salt (Enough to Cover Your Meat)

Oil (Enough to Cover Pan and Meat)

Tomato paste (Two Tablespoons)

Bouillon Cube (1)

Ossobuco (1 Large or 2 Medium Size Pieces)

UTENSILS

Pot (One Large Size)

Pots (Two Small)

Take your ossobuco and with your hands, rub all sides with rosemary, salt, oil and refrigerate overnight. Chop your onions, celery, garlic and parsley. Turn your heat on high. Take your large size pot and cover the base with oil, your bouillon cube and your onions, celery, garlic and parsley. Stir your chopped ingredients for approximately five minutes, then lower your heat and let your ingredients cook for about an hour. It is very important to make sure the onions are thoroughly cooked. When they are thoroughly cooked, they have a very soft consistency and have a brown color. Make sure they are not burnt. While the onions are cooking, take your two small pots and evenly add your chicken stock to each of your two pots. In one of them, stir in your two tablespoons of tomato paste. Bring both pots to a boil. After they have boiled put them to the side. You will need them later on. After your onions have finished cooking, put your heat on high add your ossobuco and your soup and your two tablespoons of tomato paste. Stir your ossobuco and tomato paste for about five minutes and then lower your heat and let it cook for about one hour and a half or until the meat is falling off the bone. While the ossobuco is cooking, you will add ladles of our soup from your other pot. Continue to add the soup until the pot is empty. Please know that if you do not have soup, you may use either chicken stock or water.

Simple Roast Beef

RECIPE

INGREDIENTS

Roast Beef (How Much)
Salt (To Cover Meat)
Pepper (To Cove Meat)
Olive Oil (To Cover Meat)
Celery (1 Stalk)
Carrot (½ a Carrot)
Garlic (2 Cloves)
Water (1 Cup)

UTENSILS

Pan (One Large Pan)
Pot (One Large Pot)
Fork (One)

Cover your Roast Beef with your oil, salt, and pepper and refrigerate overnight. Take your fork and brown your Roast Beef in frying pan on all sides. Take your big pot. Add your oil and water to your Large Pot. Put your heat on high and add your roast beef, celery, carrot and garlic. Keep it on high for fifteen minutes and lower your heat. Let roast beef cook twenty minutes for each pound.

Aspargus Italian Style

RECIPE

INGREDIENTS

Asparagus (1 Pound)

Garlic (3 Gloves)

Parsley (2 Tablespoons)

Olive Oil (To Cover Pan)

Soup (1 Cup)

Butter (1 Pat)

Bouillon Cube (1 Cube)

Salt (Teaspoon of Salt)

UTENSILS

Frying Pan (1)

Pot (Medium Size)

Fork

Strainer (Medium)

Begin, by finely chopping your parsley and garlic. Fill your medium pot with water and add your teaspoon of salt and your asparagus. Should you need more salt, you may always add it later. The asparagus will take between five to seven minutes to cook or until tender. You can check if they are tender, by sticking your fork into them. When they are cooked, strain them. Put them aside. Take your frying pan. Cover the bottom of it with your Olive Oil and your bouillon cube. Make sure to make your bouillon cube dissolve. When it has dissolved, add your chopped parsley and garlic and stir. Lower your flame and add your asparagus and let it sauté in the parsley and garlic. Then increase your flame and add your soup. Then lower your flame. As soon as the soup has been absorbed, your asparagus is done.

Sweet Potatoes with a Nutmeg Twist

RECIPE

INGREDIENTS

Potatoes (6 Potatoes)

Oil (Cover Potatoes)

Butter (1 Pat)

Nutmeg (2 Tablespoons)

Bouillon Cube (1 Cube)

Salt (1 Teaspoon You Can Always Add If You Need It)

UTENSILS

Pot (Medium Size)

Frying Pan (Large)

Fork (1)

Strainer (Medium)

Platter (1 Large)

Wash your potatoes and then cut them into squares. Boil them until tender. When potatoes are cut into cubes, they take less time to cook. They will probably cook between 15 to 20 minutes, but keep checking with your fork. I find that truly to be the best way to estimate if they are cooked. When they are cooked, strain them. Take your large frying pan and add enough oil to cover the pan. Put your pan on high heat and add your butter, bouillon cube. After, five minutes add your potatoes and nutmeg. Stir your potatoes with nutmeg, continue to do that until the potatoes totally absorb the flavor of the nutmeg. Serve on a platter.

Mushrooms Alla Dina

RECIPE

INGREDIENTS
Portobello Mushrooms (1 Box)
Butter (1 Pat)
Oil (To Cover the Bottom of Pan)
Garlic (1 Clover Chopped)
Parsley (5 Strains Chopped)
Bouillon Cube (1 Cube)

UTENSILS
Frying Pans (2 Medium)

Wash the mushrooms and cut. The first thing to do is to take the mushrooms and put them into the frying pan with low heat. You do this to release the water from the mushrooms. Mushrooms release a great amount of water; you need to make sure to get rid of the water before you continue with the cooking process. Add your mushroom and stir. Make sure to evenly cover your mushroom with garlic and parsley. Add your mushrooms and stir making sure to evenly cover your mushrooms with the garlic and parsley. Cook mushrooms until tender. Approximately ten minutes. Remember not to overcook them. If you do, they will have a rubbery texture. You do not want to be chewing mushroom for ten minutes before swallowing.

Tony's Peasant Potatoes

I personally love these potatoes. I could live on them! This recipe is truly peasant food. It was developed from slim pickings that were living in Tony's garden batch. Though a peasant recipe, it will compliant any plate!

RECIPE

INGREDIENTS

Celery Leaves (4 leaves shopped)

Potatoes (5)

Oil (Enough to cover potatoes)

Salt – (Enough to cover potatoes)

UTENSILS

Pot (Medium)

Spoon (Two to stir potatoes)

Small Round Dish

Take your potatoes. Peel them and wash them. Cut them into quarters. Take your medium pot. Add your water, teaspoon of salt and potatoes. Remember you will be adding salt later, so you don't need to add that much salt to the water. The potatoes should take around twenty to twenty -five minutes to cook or until tender. If you are insecure about the cooking time, you can always use your fork to check. While the potatoes are cooking, you will compose your dressing. Begin by finely chopping your celery leaves. After you chop your celery leaves, season them with your garlic, oil and salt. Stir these ingredients and pour them over your potatoes and serve.

Nonna Louisa's Cutlets

RECIPE

INGREDIENTS

Cutlets (6 pieces)

Bread Crumbs (Enough to cover cutlets)

Garlic (6 Cloves of garlic chopped)

Parsley (A Small Bunch Chopped)

Eggs (1)

Salt (1 Tablespoon)

Pepper (½ a Teaspoon)

Rosemary (½ a Teaspoon)

Blackberry Brandy (A Shot Glass)

Soup (½ A Cup)

Tomato Sauce (A Tablespoon)

Olive oil (2 Tablespoons for mixture and then enough to cover pan)

UTENSILS

Frying Pan (1 Large)

Dishes (2 Big)

Combine a mixture of your egg, two tablespoons of olive oil, and six gloves of chopped garlic, chopped parsley and rosemary. Mix all these ingredients and then have your cutlets soaked in this mixture overnight or if you are strapped for time, you can let them soak for two hours.

When you are ready to remove the cutlets, you will bread them with your bread crumbs. Then taking your frying pan and as usual coat the bottom with your olive oil. When they are cooked, you would remove them from your pan and put them aside. You would then take your frying pan and add your Blackberry Brandy, Soup and Tomato Paste bring it to a boil and add your cutlets. You would then add your cutlets and have them absorb the mixture. After the cutlets have absorbed all the ingredients, take them from your pan and serve.

Nonna Linda's Eggplant

RECIPE

INGREDIENTS

Eggplant (2 Medium Size)
Soup (½ a small pot)
Garlic (3 chopped cloves)
Bouillon Cube (½ of one)
Parsley (A Small Bunch Chopped)
Sauce (A Small Pot)
Bread Crumbs (Enough to Cover Eggplant)
(About a cup)

UTENSILS

Frying Pan

Slice your eggplant in round pieces. Place them in your frying pan, add your soup, garlic, parsley and cook until tender. After you have finished doing that, you would place your eggplant in egg wash and then bread it with your bread crumbs and then proceed to place them in your pan in layers. Between each layer of the eggplant, add your sauce and parmesan cheese and proceed to fry until your cheese has melted. When your cheese has melted, it is ready.

Louisa's Spare Rib

RECIPE

INGREDIENTS

Spare Ribs (1 Package)
Onion (1 Large Chopped)
Leek (5 Stalks Chopped)
Oil (Enough to Cover Pan)
Bouillon cube (2)
Blackberry Brandy (1 Cup To Cover Spare Ribs)
Soup (1 cup In A Pot)

UTENSILS

Frying Pan (1 Big)
Fork (1)

Begin by washing your spare ribs. Season them with your Blackberry Brandy. Cover and put them in your refrigerator. You would do this first thing in the morning. You want the spare ribs to absorb the flavor of the blackberry brandy. While they are marinating in the blackberry Brandy, proceed to chop your onions and leek. When the spare ribs have sufficiently marinated and you are ready to cook them, begin by covering the bottom of your frying pan with your oil and add your two bouillon cubes. Take your chopped onion and chopped leeks add them to your frying pan. Stir these ingredients on high heat for five minutes. Lower your heat and cover your pan and let your onions and leeks cook for about forty- five minutes. While your onions and leeks are cooking, take your soup in your pan and bring it to a boil. You want it to be hot when you put it into your spare ribs. You do this because you want it to be able to boil right away in the pan with the spare ribs. You do not want to wait for that. After the onions and leeks have completed cooking, add your spare ribs. They will need to cook for about an hour and a half to two hours. You want them to be so tender so that they come off the bone. During the cooking process, your spare ribs will become dry. Here is where your soup comes in. You will add your soup. As it dries up, you will continue to add it. This will develop into the gray for your spare ribs. After an hour and a half, you will remove your spare ribs and cover them with your gravy.

Nonna's Lentil Soup

RECIPE

INGREDIENTS

Lentils (1 Cup)

Bouillon Cube (1)

Oil (Enough to Cover Pan)

Leek (3 Stalks)

Celery (1 Stalk)

Parsley (2 Stalks)

Ham Bone (1 Bone)

Garlic (3 Cloves)

UTENSILS

Pot (One Big One)

Pot (One Medium Pot)

Spoon (One Big One)

Begin by chopping your parsley, leek, celery and garlic. After you have completed chopping them. Take your frying pan. Add your oil. Enough to cover the bottom of your pan and add your bouillon cube. Add your chopped ingredients and have them sauté in your pan for five minutes. You would then add your lentils and your ham bone. Let that sauté on high heat for about thirty minutes. While this is going on, have your water boiling in another pot on the side. After sautéing your ingredients for thirty minutes, you would then add your water. Let it boil at high heat for about fifteen minutes, then lower your heat and bring it to a slow boil. Put your cover on. Let it cook for an hour and a half.

Fried Potatoes with Rosemary

RECIPE

INGREDIENTS
Potatoes (5)

Rosemary (3 Strands)

Oil (Oil Enough to Cover Pan)

Salt (Tablespoon)

UTENSILS
Pot (Medium Size Pot)

Frying Pan (Large)

You would begin by finely chopping your rosemary. When you have completed that, you would take your potatoes and cut them in whatever way you would like. It doesn't matter for this recipe, whatever way you would like to cut them is fine. You would then take your medium-size pot and fill it with water. Add salt to your water. About a tablespoon. Add your potatoes and bring them to a boil. When they are brought to a boil. Drain them. Put them to the side. Take your frying pan. Cover your pan with the oil and add your chopped rosemary. Heat your pan for about five minutes and add your potatoes. Cook your potatoes until they are brown.

Fried Potatoes with Bay Leaves

RECIPE

INGREDIENTS

Potatoes (Five)
Bay Leaves (4)
Oil (Oil Enough to Cover Pan)
Salt (Tablespoon)

UTENSILS

Pot (Medium Size Pot)
Frying Pan (Large)

The same procedure you would use then you make it with Rosemary. You are just substituting the Bay Leaves with Rosemary.

Stuffed Mushrooms

RECIPE

INGREDIENTS

Mushrooms (1 Pound)
Onions (2 Chopped)
Garlic (4 Gloves)
Bread Crumbs (1 Cup)
Oil (Cover Pan)
Eggs (2, One Whole Egg And One Yolk)
Parmesan Cheese (½ Cup)

UTENSILS

Frying Pan (One Large)
Platter (One Large)

Chop your onions and leek. Take your frying pan. As always, make sure the bottom of the pan is totally covered with oil. Cook your onions and leeks for about 45 minutes to an hour. When your onions and leek are cooked, turn off heat and add your cup of bread crumbs and parmesan cheese. Mix well and fill your mushrooms. Put them in the oven at (300) and let cook for approximately 20 minutes or until taste.

Shrimp Alla San Micheal

RECIPE

INGREDIENTS

Shrimp (One Pound)
Garlic (5 Gloves)
Oil (To Cover Pan)
Bouillon Cube

UTENSILS

Double Boiler (One Big One)
Frying Pan (One Large)

Begin by cleaning your shrimp. Make sure you take the vein out and the shrimps out shell. Steam your shrimp in your double boiler. Steam until shrimps develop a reddish color. This should take about 10 minutes. Then strain your shrimp. Take your frying pan, as always, take your oil and make sure it covers the bottom of the pan. Then add your cube, garlic and shrimp. Cook your shrimp for an additional five to ten minutes.

Gnocchi

RECIPE

INGREDIENTS
Potatoes (6 Medium)

Three Eggs (Two Yolk and One Whole Egg)

Flour (Enough to Keep the Eggs and Flour Intact)

Salt (2 Tablespoons)

UTENSILS
Pots (2 medium)

You may begin by either baking or boiling your potatoes for about 30 to 45 minutes. But keep checking with fork until cooked. You may also microwave them which would take approximately 10 minutes. After they have cooked. Put them aside and let them cool. When they are cooled, peel them. After you have peeled them, chop them and add salt. You are going to mix your potatoes with your flour. Use enough flour so that the potatoes are able to permanently stick together. You would then roll your dough and cut it. You would form your dough into a finger form. You would then boil them. When your Gnocchi have risen to the top of your pot, they are cooked.

Sauce for Gnocchi

RECIPE

INGREDIENTS

Oil (Enough to cover pan)

Water (½ a cup)

Soup (½ a cup)

3 Pieces of Sage

Butter (Quarter of piece)

UTENSILS

1 Large Pot

Cover bottom of pot with oil. Add quarter piece of butter, Sage, Water and Soup. Let it simmer and when your butter has melted, your sauce is cooked.

Bow Tie Cookies

RECIPE

INGREDIENTS

Flour (2 Pounds)

Eggs (6) (2 Whole And 2 With Just the Yolk)

2 or 1 Stick of Butter (Ask Mom)

½ Glass of any Sweet Liquor

3 (Cups of Sugar)

Vegetable Oil (Wesson)

UTENSILS

1 Big Pot

Take your eggs, stick of butter a half glass of liquor and three cups of sugar and mix them all together with your flour. Gradually add more as you need it. Kneed your ingredients until they develop a firm consistency. When you obtain this, let your dough sit for an hour. Then you would cut your dough and put it through your pasta machine. Cut it into strips and form them into bow ties. Take your big pot and add your vegetable oil. Put your vegetable oil on medium heat. Deep fry your bowties quickly. They should have a golden color, not brown color. Lay them out on brown paper bags and pat them with bounty to release all the oil. When they have cooled sprinkle with powdered sugar.

Crostata

RECIPE

INGREDIENTS

Butter (1 Stick)

Flour (3 Cups)

Eggs (3 Yolks)

Sugar (1 Cup)

Baking Powder (1 Tablespoon)

1 Jar of Blueberry or Apricot Jelly

UTENSILS

One Long Board

1 Flat Pan

Take your long flat board. Pour your three cups of flour on your board. Crack your eggs and add them to your flour then add your cup sugar, tablespoon of baking powder and stick of butter. Kneed all your ingredients together so that develop into your dough. Take your cake pan. Grease it with your butter. Cover your pan with your dough. Leave a little dough behind to make a decoration on top of the cake. Take your Jelly and spread over the top of your dough. You would then cut your remaining dough into strips and put it diagonally on the top of the jelly. Cook in oven from forty- five to hour at 325.

Sabgione

RECIPE

INGREDIENTS
Eggs (9 Eggs)
Sugar (9 Tablespoons)
Marsala (3 Tablespoons)

UTENSILS
Bowl (Medium size)
Double Boiler

You would beat your eggs. Cook over double boiler. Cook until thick and dense. Serve it with strawberries.

Ask again.

This is for six servings

CPSIA information can be obtained
at www.ICGtesting.com
Printed in the USA
BVHW021932070720
583140BV00006B/137